A LOSING HAND

A LOSING HAND

The Human Costs of Canada's Gambling Epidemic

ROB CSERNYIK

SQ

SUTHERLAND
HOUSE

Sutherland House
416 Moore Ave., Suite 304
Toronto, ON M4G 1C9

First edition, August 2026

We acknowledge the support of the Government of Canada.

Manufactured in Canada
Cover designed by Leah Ciani and Jordan Lunn
Cover image courtesy of Alamy
Book composed by Karl Hunt

Library and Archives Canada Cataloguing in Publication
Title: A losing hand : the human costs of Canada's gambling epidemic / Rob Csernyik.
Names: Csernyik, Rob, author.
Description: First edition. | Series statement: Sutherland quarterly
Identifiers: Canadiana (print) 20260211796 | Canadiana (ebook) 20260211877 |
ISBN 9781997701750 (softcover) | ISBN 9781997701767 (EPUB)
Subjects: LCSH: Gambling—Social aspects—Canada. | LCSH: Compulsive gamblers—Canada. |
LCSH: Suicide—Canada. | LCSH: Gambling industry—Social aspects—Canada.
Classification: LCC HV6722.C3 C74 2026 | DDC 363.420971—dc23

ISBN 978-1-997701-75-0
eBook 978-1-997701-76-7

***Sutherland Quarterly*, Issue 14**
Editor – Ken Whyte
Managing Editor – Shalomi Ranasinghe
Associate Editor – Leah Ciani
Marketing Director – Krithika Chandrasekar
Publicist – Sarah Miniaci
Subscription Price: $67.99 CAD (includes HST) | Single Copy Price: $17.95 USD / $19.95 CAD
For submissions and more information, e-mail us at submissions@sutherlandhousebooks.com.

CONTENTS

PART 1

THE HUMAN COST

In the 1960s, John Hallett and his wife, Phyllis, lived in Hermitage-Sandyville, a small town on the south coast of Newfoundland, where the economy was dependent on the precarious cod industry. Searching for better lives, they moved to Canada's motor city, Windsor, where John secured a job at a Chrysler plant. "He hardly ever missed a day of work," his only child, Karlene Baert, remembers. "The man was loyal beyond belief."

Hallett was also careful with money. "He and my mom scrimped and saved all their lives," Baert says.

This financial acuity bought a brick house in the Windsor suburbs and paid for Baert's wedding and the gift of a down payment for her own family home. Hallett treated himself to a black Corvette convertible and retired mortgage-free, with savings ready to support him and Phyllis into old age.

In August 1998, Hallett, Baert, her husband, and children piled into an RV and headed back to Newfoundland. It was not the trip they had dreamed about. Hallett had looked forward to a retirement of travel and leisure with Phyllis. Newfoundland and Labrador was high on their list. But Phyllis fell ill on the cusp of this new chapter. The family pilgrimage was instead to spread her ashes after her death from congestive heart failure.

It was in Hermitage that Hallett first shared a cryptic message with Baert: one day nothing would be left for her and the family. She didn't take the comment too seriously. It was an emotional time. Baert didn't know that her father had been gambling frequently at the Windsor casino since his wife's death.

In the years that followed, Hallett's behaviour shifted in ways which worried Baert. He showed less interest in spending time with his grandkids or watching planes take off at the airport. He missed mortgage payments and drove around with expired licence tags. It was only following Hallett's first suicide attempt in 2004, when Baert realized the extent of his gambling addiction.

Based on her review of his financial records, Baert pegs his total losses at around $380,000. "He had mortgaged the home with an alternative lender, paying ridiculous rates," she remembers. With his retirement savings gone, there wasn't enough left for Hallett to gamble with. "That's when it all kind of hit him," Baert says.

Hallett moved in with his daughter's family for a while and would "lay on the couch, look at his belly, and ruminate about what he'd done," she says. Hallett also sought treatment for depression and banned himself from the casino. It continued to send him promotional offers through the mail.

On September 3, 2005, after Hallett had returned to his home, Baert appeared at his doorstep with a basket of laundry she had done for him. The house was quiet and the attic door ajar.

"I found him," she says. "I don't really like to talk too much about that."

Hallett had died by suicide at seventy-six.

While he had suffered from depression and was grieving his wife, Baert says her father's gambling "was definitely the straw that broke the camel's back." When an Ontario coroner's service investigator collected information on his death, Baert mentioned, unprompted, her father's compulsive gambling and its impact on his life. She wanted records to show "that yes, he committed suicide, but it was due to gambling."

Hallett's wasn't the first gambling-related suicide in Canada, nor was it the last.

* * *

In May 1993, Mayor Brad Woodside, visibly upset, appeared at a press conference to discuss the death of a Fredericton resident. In a small city of about fifty thousand people, there is a closeness and kinship that can make deaths resonate harder than they might in a metropolis. Stan MacNeil was a friend of Woodside's and had died by suicide at age thirty-four. He had been having trouble with video lottery terminal (VLT) addiction and had gone missing, worrying his loved ones. A week later, his body was found.

"I think the problem is much more serious than the government realizes and this is a tragedy that I don't want to see repeated in this community," Woodside said.

Yet in response to the tragedy and Woodside's appeal to reduce VLT locations to bars only, New Brunswick's finance minister, Allan Maher, made a threat. "It would mean a significant reduction in revenue to the province," Maher said. "Is [Woodside's] city prepared to absorb some of that reduction in terms of additional cuts to transfer payments from the province?"

By 1993, the machines had been regulated in New Brunswick for about three years. The province had promised to spend gambling revenue on a righteous cause: environmental clean-ups. While government regulation had reduced them by a third, there were still about 3,200 VLTs in about 2,000 locations. Woodside wasn't alone in wanting fewer VLTs. "More than 20,000 New Brunswickers have signed their names to petitions calling for curbs on the availability of the machines," reported Canadian Press.

The problem reached far beyond New Brunswick. The terminals, by now, were in every province except British Columbia and Ontario. Most provinces were relegating them to age-restricted locations, but in New Brunswick, they were still found in bowling alleys and convenience stores, in full view of anyone who might find them tempting.

Talk of environmental clean-ups funded by the machines had fallen by the wayside. Gambling was swelling the province's general revenues. "The government has literally hit the jackpot with video gambling," wrote Chris Morris of The Canadian Press. "[New Brunswick] is expecting to rake in

$33-million in much-needed revenue from the machines this year." With a $266-million deficit in 1993 and coming out of a recession, VLT profits were crucial, even if they closed only a bit of the gap.

Stan's death had made front-page news in New Brunswick, but it didn't spark deeper conversations or inspire change. A search of 1993 provincial Hansards shows only a single, fleeting mention of gambling-related suicides in a proposal to look into links between gambling and the crime rate. When the province finally removed VLTs from convenience stores later in the decade, it wasn't because they might cost lives, but because they carried the potential of normalizing gambling for children.

Nonetheless, Stan's death was a starting point. The suicide toll associated with the new wave of legalized gambling was no longer invisible. And the public had seen the timidity of political leaders when it came to protecting their communities from the worst effects of gambling, as well as the first examples of governments pushing back at the notion that their precious gambling revenues had a serious human cost.

In the past thirty years, no death attributed to gambling-related suicide, no matter how preventable the act or distressing the details, has moved a single provincial government to take meaningful, sustained action to prevent others. Hundreds of deaths like John's and Stan's have been recorded, and more still have escaped documentation. Gambling addiction treatment pioneer, Dr. Robert Custer, encountered gamblers suicidal in part because of dangers and fears stemming from illegal gambling. In 1990, he told a *Globe and Mail* columnist fixing the problem required further legalizing gambling. But Custer's vision of legal gambling was one that steered money away from criminal markets, wrote Stephen Brunt, and channeled funds "to finance research in Dr. Custer's field of expertise."

There is no shortage of evidence on the link between gambling and suicide. By the early 1990s, peer-reviewed research on the topic was increasingly common. At least once a year, the prominent *Journal of Gambling Studies* referenced it, with articles about "fruit machine" gambling in UK adolescents (1990), suicidal behaviour among Gamblers Anonymous members (1991), an evaluation of pathological gamblers in Barcelona (1992), and so on. The connection was also reported in *The Canadian Journal of Psychiatry*, in a piece which noted that 13.3 percent of pathological gamblers in Edmonton were likely to have made suicide attempts (1993). Yet suicides are a minor component of the discussions of gambling in Canada, whether among the public or lawmakers. They are often presented near the end of a laundry list of potential harms like bankruptcy and financial challenges, crime and legal issues, emotional hardships, relationship difficulties, family breakdown, and youth gambling—all of which are serious outcomes.

Governments have also failed to report how often coroners and medical examiners recorded gambling as a factor in suicides. This was true before and after the legalization of new betting innovations like VLTs. And there were no efforts to intelligently estimate how many gambling-related suicides might occur in a population when gambling options expanded. If experts working in mental health or suicide prevention had specific visions of how gambling might affect human lives, they got little public airing or interrogation in legislatures. There's no guarantee that a different approach would have changed the trajectory of gambling-related suicides in Canada, but decision-makers and the public would have had more information upon which to base their decisions about the industry, and their support for it.

Not all public officials have been ignorant of the issues. As early as 1995, when Nova Scotia prepared to open two casinos, Halifax's police chief said he expected more suicides. "We are seeing some of that social outfall already from the video lotto terminals," Vince MacDonald told Canadian Press. "The most tragic thing is when we come across a suicide note where a person has decided they cannot handle their gambling debts."

MacDonald said the police force was against casinos, concerned about their social repercussions. "Gambling of this magnitude, with this accessibility, we've never really experienced before," he said. And yet, even with the police chief of the province's largest city offering this grim assessment, politicians stayed silent. When Nova Scotia's legislature resumed in the fall, following the opening of the casinos, gambling-related suicides didn't come up.

Early on, concerns that opening casinos might increase crime rates led some communities, including Halifax, to beef up police presence through special gambling units. Halifax's unit disbanded two years later because the uptick in casino-related crime never materialized. While that prediction didn't come true, MacDonald's did.

When a Nova Scotia casino patron died by suicide in February 1998 after a ten-day gambling binge, the casino's vice-president faulted "other issues, lifestyle issues." The minutes from the next meeting of the Nova Scotia Gaming Corporation, which took place a few months later, do not address the death. Instead, board members reviewed sketches of the proposed permanent casino—oohing and ahhing over paint colours and fabric patterns.

More tragic stories started appearing across the country as gambling options increased. From the mid-1990s to mid-2000s, stories on gambling-related suicides appeared in the *Winnipeg Free Press* on an almost annual basis. For instance, there was the story of fifty-year-old "Frank" in 1996. He said he could play VLTs all day. "If a person next to me fell off his stool and had a heart attack, I wouldn't have even flinched," he said. He even "slipped out to play VLTs while his son lay in hospital in a coma, recovering from a suicide attempt over his own compulsive gambling," wrote journalist Allison Bray.

Following one man's suicide, VLTs were removed from two bars he frequented after a Manitoba Lotteries investigation revealed bar staff let him use his debit card to get cash back to play the machines. Concerns ran high after he and another Manitoban addicted to gambling committed suicide within a two-month span—six in total in the previous two years. When a known gambler went missing in January 1998, the *Free Press* reported the RCMP took the "unprecedented step" of issuing a missing persons report mentioning his gambling.

In 1997, a University of California, San Diego, study brought international attention to gambling-related suicides. It was picked up by *The Globe and Mail* and other Canadian papers. Led by sociology professor David Phillips, the study found that residents of and visitors to Atlantic City, Las Vegas, and Reno died by suicide up to four times more often than residents of or visitors to areas without legal gambling. According to *The New York Times*, the study was "the first large-scale statistical investigation of gambling and suicide."

Phillips et al. uncovered this by analyzing and comparing the estimated suicide rates in similarly sized metro areas with and without legal gambling. A city the size of Las Vegas was expected to have had 310 suicides in 1990, according to the study. Instead, it recorded 497. That same year, Atlantic City should have recorded about forty-five. Instead, it tallied sixty-four. Fifteen years earlier, before legalized gambling, Atlantic City should have still recorded forty-five suicides, but only fifty-two occurred. The study also reported that one in twenty-five Las Vegas visitor deaths was a suicide, four times the national average of one in one hundred. Atlantic City also had nearly double the national average in visitor suicides.

The authors stopped short of saying there was a direct link between suicide and gambling addiction but wrote that their data were "consistent with the hypothesis that one or more of the following subpopulations experience elevated risks of suicide": gamblers or their non-gambling spouses and children visiting gambling communities, gamblers or their non-gambling relatives who live in communities where gambling is legal, and non-gamblers who live in gambling communities and work in that industry. In short, gambling or a gambling-related factor was behind the increase in suicides.

While the executive director of the American Association of Suicidology praised the study as "quality sociological research," the president of the American Gaming Association was critical. As the *Times* reports, he "cited studies that say that people moving to the American West, where suicide rates are highest, find themselves isolated and without personal support systems and that these factors, not gambling, explain why they kill themselves."

The AGA would later commission a report which suggested—unsurprisingly, given that it's a trade association to promote gambling industry interests—that in six communities analyzed before and after the opening of casino resorts (only one of which appeared in the original study), suicides didn't increase according to their calculations.

Both studies were cited in a Canadian Public Health Association position paper, in which the CPHA said that gambling expansion was an emerging public health issue in Canada. It advocated "minimizing gambling's negative impacts while balancing its potential benefits" (such as economic development or charitable fundraising) and listed eight types of consequences of gambling, including "suicide, suicidal ideation, and suicide attempts." Among the recommendations was to advocate for "a national public policy review of gambling expansion that analyzes the effectiveness of our public ownership and accountability framework, studies the Canada-wide prevalence of problem and pathological gambling, and assesses associated health and socio-economic costs/benefits." The call went unheeded.

As the 2000s dawned, there was a tonal shift in some media coverage around gambling. Stories took on a more extreme character, and, in the days before suicide style guides suggested compassionate, sober ways to report these stories, the details were sometimes gratuitous. Yet their public airing did nothing to address what appeared to be a growing problem. In September 2000, Loto-Québec president Michel Crête responded to reports of Quebeckers dying by gambling-related suicide with sarcasm. "We hide them in the garages," he said. "We bury them in the parking lot."

Around six months later, a forty-seven-year-old man died by suicide in the parking lot of Casino de Montréal. According to the coroner's investigation report on his death, his self-exclusion period from the casino had ended the previous November and his family members suspected he had lost a large amount of money.

"What can be done?" asked *The Globe and Mail* editorial team on May 4, 2001, referencing the man's death. "A national review of the ills that stem from gambling might prove the best long-term investment." The call, again, went unheeded.

The Globe noted that gambling-related suicide statistics from elsewhere in Canada were "elusive." Part of the reason they were more prevalent in Quebec was because on multiple occasions individual coroners wrote specific warnings to Loto-Québec about pathological gambling and its link to suicide. It appears to have been more closely recorded than in other provinces. For instance, coroner Dr. Jean-François Dorval wrote of a man with a gambling addiction who "used up his financial resources" playing Loto-Québec's Banco lottery tickets. The man's family mentioned that he would buy multiple tickets from three local stores and frequently return to buy more.

Dr. Dorval thought it was necessary to draw a parallel between the sale of lottery tickets and the sale of alcohol by bar owners. Since bars have responsibilities to clients they sell alcohol to as part of their licence, ticket retailers should also have licences tied to certain responsibilities. He wrote a recommendation to Loto-Québec "with the aim of protecting human life and preventing future deaths," suggesting they teach ticket sellers how to identify people with compulsive habits and share information with them about gambling problems to "help them to identify as someone with a problem and as a person who needs help."

By 2002, a sombre milestone was reported—100 gambling-related suicides had been recorded in Quebec since the introduction of casinos and VLTs. That same year, New Brunswick lawmakers said gambling was a recorded factor in eighteen suicides since 1995. The provincial NDP leader said she suspected numbers were even higher and accused the provincial government of not doing anything about it. The public safety minister downplayed the concern, conceding that gambling was listed as a risk factor, but pointing out that other forces may have been at play.

Yet elsewhere it was largely unknown how many gambling-related suicides were coming across the desks of coroners and medical examiners, other than the occasional isolated tales.

After a regular at Hero's Pub and Eatery in Truro, Nova Scotia, committed suicide, owner Abdul Rafih learned the man had gambled away his rent money shortly before ending his life. "It's been haunting me since that day," he told reporters. Rafih removed all the VLTs from his pub, a move he estimated would cost him $30,000 in annual revenues.

Rafih was an outlier. The Restaurant Association of Nova Scotia president said most bar owners affiliated with the group wouldn't give up VLTs "without a fight because they provide significant income."

It was challenging to tie gambling to any harms because so little data existed in Canada, whether on gambling prevalence or its effects on bankruptcies, crime, hospital visits, or suicides. In the absence of data, it was easy for lawmakers and regulators to feign ignorance and downplay negative consequences by cherry-picking statistics supporting their view that legalized gambling was minimally harmful. These defences didn't always ring true. People noticed their friends and neighbours planting themselves in front of machines and exhibiting concerning gambling habits. They read the stories about suicide as calls for action. Downplaying public concerns was a kind of mass gaslighting: don't believe your own experience; gambling isn't harming anyone.

* * *

Braving the winter chill, with a small television under her arm and a receipt in her hand, Susan Piercey went on a post-Christmas mission. She left the door open behind her as she trudged through her neighbourhood in Corner Brook, Newfoundland and Labrador. This didn't surprise her parents, Keith and Catherine. Susan, a friendly blonde in her late twenties, who once scored top marks in her cosmetology program, preferred money to gifts. If she learned where an item was purchased, there was a tacit understanding that she wouldn't keep it. Either she'd return it for a refund, or sell it—sometimes for less than it was worth. The television under her arm was going to be converted to cash.

For almost a decade, Susan had been spending her time in front of different screens—the VLTs legally introduced in Newfoundland and Labrador in 1991. "To take every cent that you did earn, and waste it on those machines was something unbelievable," Keith Piercey says, estimating his daughter lost at least $100,000 over a decade of gambling. She worked three jobs at one point, sinking her paycheques into the machines in the dark corners of bars and restaurants. A student loan met the same fate. Later, to fund her addiction, she wrote bad cheques, sold items that weren't hers, and stole money from her grandmother's bank account. "They were as close as any two people could ever be," Piercey says. But when gambling addictions take over, people make decisions against their nature.

With her family's help, Susan attended residential gambling addiction treatment programs in Newfoundland and Ontario. At one facility, journal writing was part of the recovery process. Susan addressed VLTs like they were a monster lurking behind her. "If you would only let me out of your clutches and allow me to reclaim back my life, without constantly fighting to stay out of your grasp."

In another entry, she was philosophical: "I stayed and played on your empty promises and lost not only money but my soul."

In 2003, to prevent herself from gambling, Susan asked if Catherine could take control of her finances. Her mother agreed to help, but Susan never followed through. She died by suicide about a week later at age thirty-one. Susan was laid to rest in Mount Patricia Cemetery on the fringes of Corner Brook, surrounded by rolling green hills and a view of the Bay of Islands. She shares a simple grave marker with her grandmother who died in 2019.

Though stories of gambling-related suicides were becoming more common as the legalized gambling wave of the early 1990s matured, something was different about Susan's story. She was female, and young, while the subjects of many stories were male and sometimes middle-aged. She was also from Newfoundland and Labrador, a province where speaking about suicide at all was taboo.

It was only in the 1990s that Dr. Charles Hutton, the province's chief forensic pathologist, "publicly urged physicians to indicate on death certificates when a death was a clear-cut case of suicide," John Gushue wrote in the *Canadian Medical Association Journal*. Newfoundland and Labrador historically boasted an artificially low suicide rate because families and the church pressured doctors to portray the deaths as natural. Although the chief medical examiner's office and others report suicides in the province as increasing over time, there is likely an element of regression toward the mean because the deaths are being more accurately counted in recent years than in decades past. Addressing ills caused by the machines was also taboo, never mind that people were witnessing them firsthand and hearing whispers about friends, neighbours, and loved ones afflicted with gambling problems.

When the Pierceys spoke out against that backdrop in November 2003, it meant something had changed. Editorial pages struck an urgent note. "It is a horrible story, and one that should be required reading for every single Cabinet minister who has ever had a hand in the continued operation of VLTs in this province," wrote *The Telegram* in an editorial. Susan's story reached beyond Newfoundland and helped Canadians take notice of the devastation that was happening as legalized gambling matured into a major industry. It was becoming more difficult to look away from gambling-related suicides in Canada. Yet still no actions were taken by public authorities.

Most years, the Pierceys get together around the day of Susan's passing. They used to put a picture and a memorial note in *The Western Star*, but it shifted from being a paid daily paper to a free weekly a few years back. There's still a memorial mass for her annually at a local church, where the minister is a family friend.

"We never forget about Susan, but we want to forget about what happened," Keith Piercey says.

* * *

On some school days back in the late 1970s, Phillip Wong, would be excused from school by an "uncle figure," who drove with him about two hours from tiny Saint Paul, Alberta, to Edmonton, where they bet on horse races. "I was surprised to realize it later, because I was never taken on those road trips," his sister, Michelle Wong, says.

The siblings were close until their parents' 1980 divorce and started drifting apart as teenagers. Their mother eventually remarried and moved to Las Vegas. Phillip quit university to join her. He married, became a dad to twins, and opened a beauty parlour with his wife.

In 1994, Michelle visited to reconnect with Phillip and her mother, having barely seen them for a decade. Phillip's gambling habits quickly stood out. Once, Michelle was stunned to watch him lose about $500 at a casino in only a few minutes. She recalls Phillip telling his wife that he could "make" $100 USD a day if he treated gambling as a job, a common fantasy among people with problematic gambling habits.

Instead, Phillip found himself in a six-figure financial mess, losing his car and house to creditors.

As his gambling worsened, Phillip became abusive toward his wife. Some research suggests gambling addiction exacerbates coercive control and violence by male partners, although their significant others don't always connect the two, viewing gambling as a relatively innocent, unlinked hobby. It is another underexplored consequence of gambling, linked to murder-suicides in which gambling was a risk factor and the spouse who committed the murder was a gambler. At least one has been reported in Canada.

One night after a gambling binge, Phillip returned home and found his wife arguing with her ex-husband. Phillip retrieved his gun and shot the man, wounding him. Phillip landed in prison and wrote his sister hopeful letters about starting life anew once released.

After a year, US authorities offered Phillip an option to forgo further jail time in return for deportation to Canada. He returned to Saint Paul, but no longer needed to leave town to gamble. Now there were VLTs.

One afternoon in February 2000, Michelle received a voicemail about a "family tragedy." A friend had found Phillip deceased. He was thirty-six.

Alberta did not count Phillip as one of 2000's gambling-related suicides. He left no suicide note, although it might have been impossible to connect the dots even if the right questions had been asked. No statistic exists for how frequently families learn their loved one had a gambling addiction upon reviewing financial records or finding other post-mortem evidence. Coroner and medical examiner offices say families can contact them if they discover a gambling link after a suicide but that puts the burdens on the families, not the investigators.

In 2003, Michelle released the forty-eight-minute documentary, *Pieces of a Dream: A Story of Gambling*. While making the film, she learned about the extent of Phillip's gambling and linked the habit that had caused him so many troubles to his decision to die.

"The first years after his suicide were tough," Michelle says. "I actually listened to hypnosis tapes to fall asleep, because I didn't want to have that kicking around in my brain," she remembers. Her father felt the loss of his legacy; her mother filed for bankruptcy and almost lost everything. Neither parent, nor her sister, ever got over Phillip's death.

Michelle says making the film is likely the only reason she can talk about his death today. "Because I did all that crying already."

* * *

Throughout much of Canadian history, gambling was illegal. Few people faced severe gambling harms, and stories of human costs, such as suicides were rare.

Since the early 1990s, waves of legalized gambling expansion have made gambling easily accessible. All of the aforementioned examples of lives lost or ruined by gambling were from the early days of this phenomenon: before casino development ballooned, before online gambling was normalized, before the introduction of smartphones, and before the heavily advertised explosion of single-sport betting. As the industry has grown—the vast majority of it overseen by provincial governments—so has its influence. There have been well-reported positive effects on government revenues and local jobs, and less-celebrated negative effects such as addiction and suicide. Despite the sizable resources provinces have expended building and supporting the multibillion-dollar gambling industry, its negative effects remain poorly understood.

There is a simple logic about legalized gambling that is grounded in peer-reviewed research. The more accessible it becomes, the greater the severity of gambling harms, from irresponsible betting habits to mental health issues to full-blown addiction. Though debate exists about whether the expansion of legalized gambling poses greater harm to the wider public by creating new gamblers, some of whom will become addicted, or only to those gamblers already at risk for addiction, the point remains: when legal gambling expands, some people find themselves at higher risk of harms. Among this cohort are gamblers whose habits put them at greater risk for dying by suicide.

Experts suggest that gambling-related suicides comprise at least 5 to 10 percent of overall suicide figures—potentially more depending on how closely gambling is tracked as a risk factor. Not everyone accepts the data. Some argue that any suicide risk factor is too difficult to track with certainty, even if the deceased admits having gambling problems or their financial records indicate one. Others acknowledge the risk factor, but suggest that it's not possible to assign a distinct level of blame or rank to risk factors because of suicide's multi-factor nature, so it's not worth doing.

As a result, most Canadians know that gambling addiction can destroy personal and family finances, fray relationships, and cause bettors mental distress, but its most severe consequence gets less attention. A skeptical editor once asked why I referred to suicide in such a way in the context of gambling. To me it is obvious. If your relationships fray, you file for bankruptcy, you steal from an employer, and you may wind up ruined and even in prison, there is still a tomorrow. At the end of the day, you are still alive, with the possibility of recovering from and rebuilding after losses. There is no coming back from death.

About four thousand Canadians die each year by suicide, enough that the federal government has labelled suicide a public health crisis. Prevention efforts are supported by federal and provincial governments, local health authorities, individual hospitals, and such nonprofit organizations as mental health and suicide prevention helplines. In 2023, the federal government made a $156-million commitment to implement and operate a national 988 suicide crisis helpline. It is on track to answer its millionth call in 2026. Research suggests that early intervention can reduce suicides by up to a third. Countless survivors credit such intercession in their decisions to live.

Reducing suicides is a universal goal shared by governments, health practitioners, nonprofits, and society at large. Prevention advocates aim for zero suicides, or at least what is known as a "low suicide reality," but such goals are impossible without understanding and acknowledging suicide risk factors, including identifying who is at risk. That requires targeted approaches to account for the wide span of Canadians across age groups, demographics, and geographies who experience an array of concerns that make them suicidal.

In 2016, the Public Health Agency of Canada (PHAC) created a national suicide prevention strategy, identifying several groups that are disproportionately affected—LGBTQ people, men, seniors, and youth. Gamblers were not among them. The original strategy mentions only that addictions may increase suicide risk and offers gambling as an example. PHAC neglects to mention gambling in later biannual strategy updates.

PHAC media relations advisor André Gagnon says the agency recognizes the relationship between problem gambling and suicide, but that "[a]t the national level, there are limited data about problem gambling." He mentions the 2018 Canadian Community Health Survey (CCHS), a biannual survey of Canadian health habits, as a lone example. CCHS data suggests nearly one million Canadian adults—4 percent of males and 2.6 percent of females—have or are at risk for gambling problems. This puts a population equivalent to Nova Scotia at heightened suicide risks from gambling.

One of PHAC's mandates is to examine suicide rates "by groups within our communities in order to identify those who have higher rates than the global average, or have rates that are increasing more rapidly over time." The agency says no specific threshold rate determines if a group is disproportionately impacted by suicide.

At least one type of suicide governments pay close attention to—youth suicides—have been recorded at levels of about 5 percent of overall suicides in British Columbia and Ontario. Given that gambling-related suicides are believed to have similar or larger prevalence levels, they should receive at least similar attention and resources.

Some advocates suggest levels shouldn't need to be that high. When I asked an employee of Klinic Community Health in Manitoba what number of suicides with the same risk factor she considered significant, she said: "I think one percent is a significant number. If we're having conversations with folks that are having thoughts of suicide, we always need to be taking that seriously."

And yet in Canada, despite these stories being an open secret for generations, we aren't paying them any mind.

PART 2

HOW WE GOT HERE

On December 29, 1989, at the Crystal Casino in Winnipeg, Manitoba, about three hundred prospective players stood around, elbow-to-elbow, eager for action. It was opening night and the table games, which included baccarat, blackjack, and roulette, were packed.

One attendee waiting to play blackjack at a table with $2 minimum bets told the *Winnipeg Free Press* he was "terribly disappointed" at waiting two hours without being dealt a single card. The casino was dry, so he couldn't even sip beer while standing around. The only shortcut was upping the ante. In a section called La Mezzanine, tables with $100 minimum bets sat empty for two hours after opening.

Provincial governments and starry-eyed business people had begun mulling the launch of permanent, commercial operations like the Crystal Casino as soon as the federal government legalized lotteries in 1969. One of the first proposals wanted to establish a jumbo jet airport in rural Picton, Ontario, with a casino open only to travellers. Some provinces investigated the viability of casinos within their borders. One Nova Scotia report in the 1970s posited casino resorts studding the coastline could be lucrative, but the idea was premature. At the time, only Las Vegas offered destination casinos in North America. Reports from Quebec suggested that the industry, if not handled appropriately, might harm residents more than it would benefit them. Balance was necessary.

Charity casinos popped up for special events, and struck a balance by offering a minimalist, unglamorous take on gambling. They were designed as fundraising tools, not as foundations of a significant economic engine. Most were open for defined time periods and then disappeared until the next fundraiser. Winnipeggers grew accustomed to one at the monolithic convention centre, about ten minutes by foot from the Fort Garry Hotel. For several weeks annually, players would make small wagers while breathing in second-hand smoke. Keen to increase Fort Garry's occupancy rate and profits, the owner courted the province with discounted rent. It reportedly cost $100,000 less to lease space for a full year in the grand limestone hotel than the government was paying for a few months at the convention centre. With this bargain sweetening the financial equation, Canada made the leap from low-profile, short-term charity casinos to its first year-round, government-run commercial casino.

The year prior to the Crystal's opening, speakers at an international gambling symposium in British Columbia anticipated "a shift away from welfare-oriented (charity) gambling to gambling in the name of profit," wrote Colin Campbell in his survey of legal gambling in Canada. There was a fiscal logic to it. Part of the Crystal's aim was attracting tourists and recapturing gambling dollars that the Manitoba government believed were being spent out of province. The minister responsible for lotteries promised to spend his gambling profits on a good, clean cause: "Reforming and improving such areas as health promotion, disease prevention, improved technology, new equipment and alternatives to existing health care services throughout Manitoba."

Early on, anonymous letters, supposedly authored by Crystal Casino employees, were left at media outlets across Winnipeg. They alleged that slots had been altered to increase the odds of players winning, then reset several days later to attract "the suckers." The Manitoba Lottery Foundation denied the allegation. Multiple assessments, including those by the Addictions Foundation of Manitoba and the CCHS, have since recorded Manitoba as having some of Canada's highest rates of people with, or at risk for, gambling problems. Mostly, however, the Crystal Casino was considered a success. It quickly brought in a tidy annual profit of $8 million against a cost of about $5 million to open.

Other provinces took notice of the Manitoba experiment, and stories from the United States, where casinos were increasingly proposed as economic development tools. Tired economies like Atlantic City, New Jersey, and Deadwood, South Dakota, and Tunica, Mississippi had legalized gambling between the late 1970s and early 1990s. They were drawing tourists who injected new money into local economies, creating jobs and boosting tax revenues. New large-scale casinos would follow in Quebec, Ontario, Nova Scotia, and Saskatchewan.

* * *

In *At Odds: Gambling and Canadians, 1919-1969*, McGill University history professor Suzanne Morton writes that Canadians were ambivalent toward gambling for much of the twentieth century. The policy was "unofficial toleration and official condemnation," with Protestants among the loudest opponents. But their Puritan belief that "it was wrong to encourage 'something for nothing' at the expense of thrift and savings" became increasingly unpopular as Canadians embraced activities like bingos, horse racing, and raffles, Morton observes.

As Canadians did so, law enforcement was put in a tricky situation, writes Colin Campbell. "Policing authorities through the twentieth century often found themselves stymied by the ironic situation of willingly turning a blind eye to formally illegal bingos and raffles organized, conducted and participated in by upstanding members of their communities," he writes. "Consequently, police authorities in Canada clamoured for greater clarity in the criminal law pertaining to gambling generally."

Other than permitting betting on horses and some games of chance, laws dated back to the first Criminal Code from 1892, which was itself inspired by centuries-old English statutes.

This was ancient history compared to the shift in Canadian attitudes toward gambling identified by Campbell and co-author Garry Smith. "Since the mid-1960s, notions of gambling generally and excessive gambling specifically have been reconstructed," they write in a 2003 Canadian Bulletin of Medical History research paper. "Gambling, if done in moderation, is today generally viewed as an acceptable form of leisure."

People still held concerns about the role of organized crime, that gambling bled earnings and savings dry and could cause tumult in families. It also offended the personal moral and religious codes of some Canadians, though their numbers were flagging. By 2002, a Leger Marketing survey reported that only 41.4 percent of Canadians surveyed found gambling immoral. The most irksome act according to nearly 90 percent of poll takers? Shoplifting.

Campbell and Smith describe a movement "from vice to disease to responsibility" in social perceptions of gambling. Historically, those who experienced gambling losses were considered "derelict, immoral or criminal," but over time this came to be viewed as a health problem requiring "government-sponsored therapeutic intervention." Yet even as governments offered therapy, they dodged the blame for their role as croupier. As the idea that gambling could be enjoyed responsibly gained wide acceptance, excessive gambling became a personal problem, not the fault of the society that enabled it. "The responsible gambling paradigm transposes social problems affiliated with excessive gambling into individual problems and depoliticizes them," Campbell and Smith argue.

The gambling landscape first started to take on its modern character in 1969, when the federal government legalized lotteries to fund government projects such as hosting the 1976 Montreal Olympics. These were mostly small-scale, targeted initiatives, with relatively moderate prize money offered. Canada's first national lottery, Lotto 6/49, started in 1982. Players picked a six-number combination once a week in pursuit of $500,000 jackpots—an attention-getting sum but less than 1 percent of today's larger prize pots. Lotteries were taking off across North America. Newspapers published trend pieces on lottery tickets, and draws became must-see TV. It was a neat fit with the 1980s culture of excess, when *Lifestyles of the Rich and Famous* introduced the world to luxury porn and became a ratings hit. Playing lotto was a chance to win your way into the wealthy elite, or at least daydream about it until the numbers were picked.

Between the early 1980s and early 1990s, lottery ticket revenues tripled. Governments still wanted more. A Western Canada Lottery Corporation spokesperson told the *Calgary Herald* in 1990 that with two-thirds of Canadian adults playing lotteries, increasing revenues required new twists. Soon consumers were offered new sports lottery tickets, known as Proline and Sport Select. Players selected at least three correct sports game outcomes in what's called a parlay bet. The bigger the wager, and the more outcomes the player correctly predicted, the more money they won. "It's a completely different product and we're hoping it will attract a new segment of the marketplace, and that would be the sports enthusiast," the WCLC spokesperson said.

Canadians were already betting on the ponies, but to this point the only way to bet on major sports leagues in Canada had been through the grey market. In 1990, Curtis Stock of the *Edmonton Journal* reported estimates that sport wagers across North America totalled a staggering $20 billion. Only about $1.3 billion of that was wagered legally in Nevada, the major exception to blanket prohibitions on sports betting. The leagues themselves were against the legitimization of sports betting. "We have always opposed any lottery operation which is in any way dependent on the scores of NHL games," the National Hockey League's legal counsel and vice-president told media. Sports team owners worried that betting would taint the wholesomeness of sporting events, overshadow the games themselves, and lead to match fixing. Leagues didn't want to be responsible for influencing child fans to gamble.

But governments wanted the revenue. They overruled the leagues to introduce their sports lotteries. The British Columbia Lottery Corporation president told league officials that lotto funds helped build community rinks that fostered future NHL prospects. When the NHL said using team names was infringing on their copyrights, lotteries used the city names instead. The tickets quickly spread across all provinces. Hockey's most popular broadcaster, Don Cherry, appeared in ads hawking the lotteries. The idea was still shocking enough that one writer for Vancouver's *The Province* cheekily suggested governments go all in on vice. "It is only a small leap from alcohol to drugs, as so many of us know already. Imagine:

a kind of scratch 'n' sniff thing for cocaine. Or a Lotto Crack-o. Or, moving into other areas, Lotto Hook-o. Or Gigol-o, not to leave out the women," wrote columnist Jeani Read.

When the NBA was looking at expanding to Toronto in the early 1990s, its commissioner, David Stern, hesitated because he wanted the league removed from Proline's offering in Ontario. "We don't like to see people encouraged to bet the grocery money on the outcome of any sport . . . but particularly our own," Stern told media. But the callout did nothing to chasten the government and talks stalled. Public support for the NBA position didn't change government minds either. One survey of Toronto area residents found nearly 80 percent wanted to drop the NBA from Proline, and 64 percent believed that the economic spinoffs from the NBA team outweighed what the province would recoup from the lost Proline wagers. Ultimately, money talked. The league offered millions to support government initiatives like health and tourism in exchange for OLG wiping basketball from Proline tickets. It wouldn't return until 2016.

* * *

As these paper games and casinos were expanding, legalized gambling was also pushing into the deeper and, experts say, more dangerous territory of electronic gambling machines. Video lottery terminals and slot machines are addictive by design. Even ignoring the research, anyone who has played the machines for a short time understands how this is true, and gamblers who develop addictions understand it best. To keep players wagering, game rhythms are hypnotic. There are lights and sounds and increasingly sophisticated (nearly infinite) combinations of rewards. Players are offered free spins and bonus games. They endure near misses in pursuit of "winning" a jackpot. Losses get disguised as wins and sometimes, as money runs out, a bonus is tossed their way to keep them in the game. These traits led VLTs to earn nicknames such as "the devil's television" and "the crack cocaine of gambling."

That government-owned gambling industries would make VLTs ubiquitous sounds like a conspiracy theory, but it's not. From their humble start in New Brunswick in 1990, tens of thousands of VLTs were plugged in for play three years later in all provinces but British Columbia and Ontario. Over the years, those two provinces have demonstrated lower rates of gambling addiction than elsewhere in Canada.

In Atlantic Canada, the machines had an outsized effect, particularly in Newfoundland and Labrador, where the provincial economy was upended by the early 1990s cod moratorium, putting about thirty thousand fishers and plant employees out of work. Clyde Wells, NL premier between 1989 and 1996, said three times in one interview that legalizing VLTs was his biggest mistake. "If I had my time back I would never permit VLTs in the province," he said in 2020. Some bars turned into mini casinos with twenty machines, skirting regulations that permitted only five. The province stopped short of getting rid of the machines, but outlawed land-based casinos. Today it remains the only province without one.

Nevertheless, by the end of 2000, there were about thirty casinos nationwide, a number that has grown to about 100 today. Though drawing tourists was ostensibly part of the plan, most of the money comes from local players. Some casinos opened in communities high-rolling tourists were unlikely to visit and lacked the amenities to attract them—from gourmet restaurants and high-end spas, to upscale hotels and shopping arcades.

With the physical gambling realm having undergone a dramatic redefinition, the next metamorphosis started taking shape online. Grey-market offshore casinos started to appear online as the millennium dawned and just over half of Canadians age fifteen and over were using the internet. Everything online was in its infancy, including chasing the high-stakes thrills of in-person play discreetly out of public view on home computers. Players could bet and play games any time of day, including virtual versions of slot machines, blackjack, and poker.

Despite being registered in far-flung places such as the Caribbean or the Isle of Man, the sites remained illegal and unregulated in Canada. Players logging on didn't know or care. A Canada West Foundation report proposed that the problem was best ignored. "It is not clear that a reasonable market for Internet-based gambling in Canada exists, nor is it clear that such a market could be created," wrote Robin Kelley, Peter Todosichuk, and Jason Azmier in 2001. The think tank argued that in trying to capture and regulate these players, governments might inadvertently create wider demand for online gambling.

The grey market grew as internet adoption increased and the number of websites expanded. Eventually, as "dumb" phones gave way to smartphones, people started gambling on downloaded applications as well as over web browsers. Provinces decided the market was a threat, not only to citizens but to their revenues. They responded by launching their own legal, government-owned online casinos. British Columbia Lottery Corporation launched the first in North America on its Play Now site in 2010. A CBC reporter wrote, "the province wants to recover the estimated $100-million BC residents spend on illegal online gambling websites operated offshore." Today these sites exist in all provinces (but no territories).

Betting limits would not appear out of place in a VIP lounge. Players can wager up to a $250 maximum bet on one blackjack hand in Atlantic Lotto's online casino. Since three hands can be played at once, gamblers can lose $750 in a few card flips. On British Columbia Lottery Corporation's PlayNow.com, some online table games have eye-popping $10,000 maximum bets. Despite how far these games have strayed from the original aim of legalizing gambling to capitalizing on it, there was still further to go, as we'll discuss. Continuous expansion has reshaped the Canadian gambling industry into a juggernaut with $150 billion wagered annually.

* * *

Government appetite for gambling caught experts off guard. In a 1995 speech, casino researcher and University of Nevada, Las Vegas professor Bill Thompson predicted little significant casino expansion in Canada. He believed the revenues and the number of jobs they provided were too small for provinces to bother. Thompson also doubted governments would give up certain protections that made Canadian casinos different from American ones. "They are unlikely to promote liquor consumption, to abandon dress codes, to establish credit gaming to a large degree, [and to] engage in giving major complimentary items to many players." He noted that Windsor, Ontario, at the time, was the only Canadian casino without closing hours, "and [casinos] will continue to have these." But except for large-scale credit gaming, provinces dropped these rules as the industry expanded, choosing marketability and revenues over harm minimization.

It's a misnomer to call the discourse around legalized gambling expansion in Canada "debates." The term suggests two-sided conversations, robust arguments examining the other side's points and, ultimately, the strongest case prevailing. Instead, the chatter around gambling in Canada is one-sided, with the pro-gambling side barreling over opposition and declaring victory, sometimes aided by specious talking points. Valid critiques are discounted as rooted in bad faith, misunderstanding, or malice.

There has been little fierce, sustained pushback to gambling expansion from opposition politicians, advocates, or the public. It flares up only occasionally, with concerns quickly dispatched by lawmakers. "In both the United States and Canada," said Thompson in another speech in the early 1990s, "political leaders seek to sneak gaming in through backroom legislative and council deals where it can be found that industry participants—Las Vegas operators and gaming vendors—have very adequate access, but American and Canadian citizens are totally blocked out." He referenced a lack of casino gambling referendums and the issue's absence in political campaigns in Manitoba, Ontario, or Quebec. "Yet all three governments endorsed casinos," he added, noting similar patterns in the United States. What resistance exists is left mostly to scattered anti-gambling activists.

Aside from a few scattered referendums on VLTs more than two decades ago—including province-wide in New Brunswick and local affairs in several Alberta communities—legalized gambling expansion has been a top-down decision pushed on citizens. Governments decided they wanted more gambling and crafted narratives to sell the public on their grand designs, rather than balancing their ambitions with public consensus.

As Saskatchewan prepared to launch a large casino in Regina, MLA Bill Boyd moved a motion in 1995 that a referendum on gambling expansion was necessary and should be held alongside the next provincial election. "Do the people of Saskatchewan support expanded gambling? It's never been asked," he said in the legislature. "Before there's any more harm done with gambling in this province, we should ask that fundamental question of the people of this province. Do they want gambling or not?" The next day, MLA Lynda Haverstock commented that "not one of 53 members of the government side stood and said one word on behalf of their constituents." No referendum ever came to pass. The casino opened and several more in the province followed.

In Nova Scotia, residents were quick to associate VLTs with negative social effects. A government-run survey suggested they also disliked the idea of Nova Scotia opening casinos. A petition asking lawmakers not to forge ahead with gambling palaces attracted fifty thousand signatures. Yet the government went ahead. Former Sydney mayor turned Liberal MLA Manning MacDonald admits he had doubts. "I was torn between the people in my constituency who didn't want the casino for a number of reasons, and those who wanted the jobs, no matter what they looked like." Unemployment in Sydney was about 25 percent at the time, the same as the height of the Great Depression. The casino promised a few hundred new jobs in the community, not to mention others during construction. There were also hopes it might act as a tourist magnet, creating further hospitality and tourism job spinoffs. MacDonald said he didn't express his doubts publicly because, as part of a caucus, "you're either there or you're not." He supported other job creation ideas like developing the film industry. While nobody pushed back against movies, "everybody railed against the casino coming here," MacDonald says.

Bernie Boudreau, Nova Scotia's finance minister at the time, was considered the casino's champion. He says even the firms bidding to manage Nova Scotia's new casinos didn't want to build in Sydney. "A number of them very clearly expressed a reluctance to do that," he said. They only wanted to open in the more attractive Halifax market. A Sydney casino was the province's idea, not only to create jobs, but to generate money for charities and for First Nations. The latter were offered revenue agreements in exchange for cracking down on grey-market VLTs in their communities, and not opening their own casinos. MacDonald recalls area MLAs having little discussion with Boudreau about the casino. "It was announced and done," he says. "And we were all there dutifully standing around the ribbon cutting."

Within its first few years of operations, Sydney casino's low revenues led to lower than expected payments to First Nations and rumours of closure. The province nixed the charitable contribution in 1999, reallocating $1.6 million worth of undistributed funds to general government revenues.

After leaving office, MacDonald defended the Sydney casino in a *Cape Breton Post* op-ed: "The jobs are welcomed and twenty years later the sky has not fallen over Sydney." He's not wrong, but once the casino is built, the jobs that remain are mostly lower-earning hospitality jobs, and 15 percent of Nova Scotia's casino workforce was cut within the first few months of operation. By 2019, the Halifax and Sydney casinos retained only 64 and 35 percent of their workforces, respectively.

Conclusions like MacDonald's are one of the reasons serious interrogation of gambling's outcomes seldom happens in Canada. "The sky isn't falling" is a low bar, but an effective message for a public which once feared their communities would explode with additional crime and vices and have their character irreparably damaged. It's a message that comes up again and again each time the industry expands. Negative repercussions are felt, the original promises aren't fully delivered, yet the worst fears never come to pass. The benchmark for success remains low.

Even a protest tied in with a hit television show couldn't make a difference. On a 2005 episode of *Trailer Park Boys*, the character Bubbles (with the trademark Coke-bottle glasses) talks about Ray, a local resident addicted to playing VLTs. Bubbles mentions that Ray always thinks he comes out ahead. It wasn't another punchline. It was meant to provoke.

The late actor John Dunsworth, who played the show's main antagonist, Mr. Lahey, had spoken publicly about his VLT addiction. He lost "thousands" to the machines. Dunsworth used his fame to be part of a broader conversation about the issue, supporting a related story arc on

Trailer Park Boys, narrating a video about gambling addiction, and adding his voice to an activist campaign to fight VLTs in his home province.

Halifax MLA and former provincial Liberal leader Danny Graham, together with Dunsworth and other concerned individuals, formed an advocacy group called GameOverVLTs. Debbie Langille, a former fraud investigator for the federal government was a core member of the group. She was in recovery from VLT gambling. Within three years of first playing, she filed for bankruptcy after gambling away about $160,000, half of it from her RRSPs and savings.

Graham said the group had three primary goals. "First, we intend to educate Nova Scotians about the uniquely destructive impact of VLTs on Nova Scotia families. Second, we will help families find the support they need." The third goal was to "campaign for the eventual elimination of these machines from Nova Scotia."

Calling for the elimination of the entire industry was bold. Even MADD, which aims to reduce impaired driving accidents and deaths, doesn't call for the eventual elimination of alcohol. The trouble was that the nearly 3,850 VLTs sprinkled across Nova Scotia were big business, not only for the province's gaming corporation, which generated $200,229,000 in net revenues for the 2004–05 fiscal year from the machines, but for the VLT hosts who shared in the revenues.

The Nova Scotia government wasn't about to surrender. Several days before the initial GameOverVLTs press conference, where Graham outlined its goals, the province released "A Better Balance," a report with twenty-three recommendations to reshape the province's gaming industry. These included senior and youth education programs, slowing VLT play, and adding more resources to treat "problem gambling" based on residents' needs.

Public officials were generally far removed from the real-world consequences of gambling addiction, and the province was compromised by its dependence on gambling revenues. GameOverVLTs knew the downsides of gambling intimately. Some members had lost loved ones or experienced suicidal thoughts themselves because of their gambling. In 2007, Langille told *The Coast*, a weekly alternative newspaper in Halifax, that she was casually tracking gambling-related suicides and had learned of fifteen over a period of about three years.

"A Better Balance" proposed a half measure, or, rather, a quarter measure, reducing the VLT count by 1,000—800 that November and 200 further by attrition in future years. Nova Scotia Premier John Hamm defended the machines by claiming that regulated VLTs prevented illegal ones from entering the market. An Ontario Provincial Police detective rejected the notion in a 2005 *Globe and Mail* interview. He said grey-market machines make too much money for owners to disappear entirely. "Legalizing it doesn't help and just makes it worse by breeding more gambling addicts," the detective said. "If they're not around, a lot of people will never go find them. It's better to have none."

GameOverVLTs continued on for several years before eventually admitting defeat. Not long after Langille died from illness in 2014, the website disappeared and the group dispersed. In 2022, three actors portraying their Trailer Park Boys characters, including Bubbles, appeared in an ad for the newly legal sportbook website PointsBet Canada. Danny Graham, asked for reflections on his time as an anti-VLT activist, declined. "I have not been involved in this issue for fifteen years and frankly don't believe my comments on this matter would be informed," he said. After leaving politics, he worked as chief engagement officer for a nonprofit and counsel to a major regional law firm headquartered in Halifax. One of the firm's clients happens to be the Atlantic Lottery Corporation.

Still other ill-fated protests have tried the legal route. There have been several attempts at class-action lawsuits, including one involving Susan Piercey's family. In 2007, the Pierceys sued the Atlantic Lottery Corporation (ALC). The class counsel, St. John's lawyer Ches Crosbie, was moved by reports of gambling-related suicides. "It happens, and no one doubts it happens," he says. "That's what got me interested."

Crosbie, who was Newfoundland and Labrador's Progressive Conservative Party leader from 2018 to 2021, says the key problem is that VLTs, as was alleged in his lawsuit, are programmed to be played continuously rather than with built-in session limits. That may be fine for some casual players, but for others it can foster addiction and result in significant losses. "Governments could address it," he says, "but they've got their hand too deep in the cookie jar."

He tried suing ALC under the Trade Practices Act, but the Newfoundland and Labrador Supreme Court struck down that approach, saying the Crown corporation was immune. With Susan Piercey's estate serving as lead plaintiff, a second lawsuit was filed alleging that ALC's VLTs are inherently addictive. After the court ruled a deceased individual's estate couldn't lead a class action, new lead plaintiffs replaced the Pierceys. "It was just such a relief to get away from that," Keith Piercey says. "We just didn't want to be involved anymore because it wasn't going anywhere. That can be discouraging, and you don't want to keep on fighting." He also feels, in retrospect, that the lawsuit's objective was about compensation more than the change he wanted, then and now—a ban on VLTs.

Attempts to proceed with the case sputtered for a few more years before being halted by a 2020 Supreme Court of Canada decision that favoured ALC and the other defendants in a five-to-four vote. Over the next two years, each Atlantic province outlawed class actions against the lottery corporation, including Newfoundland and Labrador in November 2021. Backdated to the 1992 launch of the NL Lotteries Act, the manoeuvre shields the ALC and provincial governments from group lawsuits.

Crosbie says individuals can still sue, but it can be more challenging, at least in part due to "hundreds of thousands of dollars" in legal fees required. The legislation also prevents plaintiffs from suing the ALC for punitive damages—the financial penalties which express community disapproval and punish and deter behaviours a court finds harmful. Defendants can request compensation only for income loss, pain and suffering, or other harms.

"It's all rigged against the individuals," Crosbie says.

* * *

The lawsuits highlight one of the unique features of gambling operations in Canada: government ownership. In the United States, state governments regulate casinos; they don't run or own them. In Canada, provinces do it all through Crown gaming or lottery corporations, run at arm's length. That makes them especially difficult to fight. Governments get the benefit of the doubt over, say, corporations, and the state has virtually unlimited resources to defend itself against protest actions, not to mention the capacity to simply pass laws to shield itself from accountability.

These gaming corporations were initially developed to solve a public problem, which gave them a certain legitimacy. VLTs, for instance, were proliferating outside the law, making citizens and governments uneasy. "These illegal machines had no age restrictions and were located in restaurants, service clubs, garages, bars, convenience stores, and shopping malls. Neither payouts nor the size of bets were regulated. Credit and cheque cashing were thought to be common occurrences," wrote HLT Advisory, a hospitality, leisure, and tourism consultancy, in a report on Canadian VLT history.

There was a demonstrable need for a fix. According to HLT's report, there were up to seven thousand illegal VLTs operating in New Brunswick alone when it started regulating the machines in 1990. Governments felt they could drain the swamp, so to speak. But first, they had to sell the public on the concept of being a slot machine operator.

Two key arguments were used. First, the provinces noted that when players wagered outside a regulated market, the economic benefits of gambling flowed to sometimes illegal operations in foreign jurisdictions. They wanted to keep the money within their borders. Second, a regulated gambling market would crush grey market (unregulated, but otherwise not criminal) and black market (criminal-run) enterprises, and shift customers to supposedly safer province-run establishments. Lawmakers have applied these arguments to all types of gambling expansion over time, including lotteries, land-based casinos, parlay sports tickets, government-owned online gambling, single-sport betting, and iGaming expansion. But VLTs were the training ground for the pitch.

"Regulatory resistance" is a recognized phenomenon in gambling research. Some politicians, moral critics, public-health advocates, and religious groups will oppose government involvement in gambling citing community and individual harms. Proponents respond with a narrative of their own, citing the perils of unregulated gambling markets, the rights of consumers to gamble if they want, the economic benefits derived from regulated gambling, and so on. Related to this is what Bill Thompson called the strategy of "guarding the border," with the goal of keeping "daily and weekly" gamers playing in their home markets.

Outflows were central to the sales pitch for government-owned casinos, VLTs, and other gambling in Canada. Ontarians were told their economy lost $600 million a year at American casinos when their province was pitching a Windsor-based gambling palace. Manitoba estimated its pockets were $100 million lighter when pushing the Crystal Casino. In 1991, Quebecers heard the province was losing $135 million to gambling outflows.

These totals shock residents and make headlines, but they're rarely explained. Details such as how many gamblers are counted, or how their average spend is calculated, or what portion of that spend is actually dependent on gambling are usually missing. One exception is a study out of Michigan, which was considering casino gambling in the early 1990s. A leisure and resort company estimated that $416 million USD flew out of Detroit's airport annually, headed for Atlantic City and Las Vegas. That comprised air fares, entertainment, hotels, and meals for about ten thousand weekly departures. The implication was that $416 million would have been spent locally if gambling were available in Michigan. Realistically, some proportion of those travellers would have taken those trips anyway.

The figures cited by provincial governments do not bear scrutiny. Given that provinces had reasonably similar gambling offerings and participation rates, some correlation should have existed between outflows and population size. But Quebec, with seven times more residents than Manitoba, projected only $35 million more in gambling outflows. Ontario, with almost ten times more residents than Manitoba, reported a whopping six times its outflows. This faulty arithmetic also assumes the same direct substitute effect as the Michigan study—that players would sink all, or at least a significant portion, of their outside-market spending into the legal, local alternative.

Today, similarly dodgy figures are used to pitch online gambling expansion. Often this is measured through user surveys or web traffic patterns, rather than specific spending data or playing habits. Concrete details such as the number of active, unregulated player accounts are considered proprietary, competitive business information and not released.

There has been little discussion of the purpose and operations of lottery corporations since they were launched several decades ago to solve specific public problems. It's not for lack of issues worth discussing, starting with "what is a lottery corporation for?" On its surface, a lottery corporation is meant to conduct and manage gaming operations. But should its performance be measured on revenue growth like a Fortune 500 corporation? Or should it be considered a public service that only needs to sustain itself? Should government-owned gambling offer the same level of products and perks as a Vegas casino, or something more rudimentary? Should government-owned gambling services be advertised around the clock like breakfast cereals, or should their branding and promotion be constrained as with cigarettes and other products known to cause public harms? If the growth of gambling means more lives ruined, is there a point where a government-linked organization will draw a line on harm reduction grounds, forgone profits be damned? Are there better ways for governments to fund their general revenues? None of these questions has had an adequate hearing, and none has a clearly defined answer decades into the gambling expansion.

* * *

All of the above happened before the tsunami of gambling options that hit Canada over the last decade. People no longer require physical gambling opportunities at casinos or bars or corner stores—new digital options allow them to legally gamble at all hours of the day, at home, at work, at school, in the bathroom, or anywhere else. Simultaneously with these developments, sports gambling moved from the shadows to centre field.

Fantasy sports betting boomed in the 2010s. Companies like DraftKings and FanDuel became massive while operating in a grey area. The Unlawful

Internet Gambling Enforcement Act banned American financial firms from processing payments from or to certain types of gambling companies, but fantasy sports, where players select their favourite players from across a league and "teams" compete based on real-world player performance, weren't subject to the act. Over the decade, the likes of DraftKings and FanDuel built a market, partnerships with leagues, and the infrastructure that made classic sports betting on single-game outcomes, point spreads, goal scorers, and so on, all but inevitable. The United States opened the door for states to allow so-called single-game sports betting in 2018. Canada followed in 2021. Ontario immediately launched a digital sportsbook called Proline+. Now available in all provinces through their respective lottery corporations, these digital sports books allow players to make bets before or during matches using a web browser or a smartphone app. Demand was high from the start. Before its first week of operations ended, Proline+ processed more than $1 million in bets in Ontario.

In 2022, Ontario launched an iGaming industry, officially allowing privately owned online casinos—including those previously operating outside Ontario law—to be licensed in the province and subject to certain regulations including "responsible gaming" requirements. In return, the casinos are permitted to market their websites to the public. They pay the Ontario government a 20 percent tax on revenues.

In only a few years, iGaming has become a massive industry in Ontario with forty-four operators running seventy-seven websites as of May 2026. More than two million user accounts have been opened; a recent count of active accounts was closer to 1.3 million. A consultant's report commissioned by casino operator Great Canadian Entertainment suggested that Ontario's government-sanctioned casinos could lose $550 million annually from gamblers flocking to iGaming from the in-person casinos, which the government earns a bigger cut of revenues from. The switch is no doubt at least partly responsible for Ontario casino revenues falling below target in fiscal 2023–24 by almost that amount.

These developments were unfathomable twenty or thirty years ago. The barriers were too high. Professional sports leagues would have to discard their long-held worries about betting corrupting the sanctity of their games. Governments would have to permit marketing on a grand scale with few restrictions. And gaming corporations would have to steer away from more profitable in-person gambling options for a smaller share of the larger online pie. Yet this is our reality.

Ontario has joined the top five North American online gambling markets, elbowing past many US states that have been in the business longer. A report prepared for the government expected iGaming to mature gradually over several years. Instead, it exploded out of the gate. A Deloitte consulting report, commissioned by iGaming Ontario, says the market's economic contribution to Ontario's GDP was equivalent to $2.7 billion in fiscal 2023–24. These economic impacts are touted by the Ontario government as a win and have inspired a copycat.

The Alberta government launched an iGaming market in July 2026 modelled on Ontario's, just in time to bet on the World Cup. The minister in charge of iGaming, Dale Nally, told a gaming summit that he heard up to seventy operators wanted to enter the market. Lobbyists are already pushing for an iGaming market in BC, but to date the government says it isn't interested. The Quebec Online Gaming Coalition, which includes member companies Bet99, DraftKings, and Flutter, has been lobbying for an iGaming market since May 2023. The Crown corporation in charge of gambling, Loto-Québec, is pushing back. "One thing must be set straight: the only Quebec-related aspect of the Quebec Online Gaming Coalition is its name," a Loto-Québec spokesperson told a gambling news website in February 2026. "It brings together foreign companies that do not create value in Quebec." Only time will tell how the trend will grow.

The promotional blitz for these new forms of gambling is unyielding and omnipresent—from sports matches themselves to billboards to jerseys to social media. Ads are on sports radio, podcasts, even dating apps like Grindr. Sports stars like Wayne Gretzky and Connor McDavid pitch bettors during commercial breaks. Unscrupulous content creators and influencers post breathlessly about online casinos and sports books, including, in some cases, how to take pricey (and dubious) online classes to learn how to beat the house.

Matthew Young, chief research officer of Greo Evidence Insights, says that despite the expansion of gambling in Canada, the rate of gambling addiction has been "pretty stable" for about twenty years. It's been like alcohol or cannabis where some people experience problems, but severe harms are generally "contained and managed." Yet a 2024 poll from Mental Health Research Canada (MHRC) suggests the push into online and single-sport betting may have changed this. It reports about 10 percent of Canadians are at high risk of gambling problems, with the number rising to about 20 percent among Canadians aged eighteen to thirty-four. "These are astonishing numbers," says Young. A 2012 review of gambling prevalence surveys found only 0.4 to 8.1 percent of people had gambling problems. Young cautions that the MHRC numbers may be inflated because the sample is drawn from an online panel, yet it still feels like a warning to him. If the newer numbers are even roughly accurate, gambling problems may have become dramatically more widespread than ever before.

The vast expansion of government-led gambling options appears to have exhausted its opponents. Levels of public protest have fallen sharply. When government-owned casinos and video lottery terminals were launched in the 1990s, citizen activists, faith groups, opposition politicians, and small businesses railed against the expansion. An Ontario MPP left his caucus over casino legalization. Today, gambling is accessible everywhere. The fundamental problems identified by critics of government-run gambling—the addictive nature, the damage to families and relationships, financial hardships, and the disproportionate impact on non-white or economically disadvantaged individuals—still remain. Yet public pushback has mostly disappeared.

One of the few signs of displeasure with the new environment is the activist group Ban Ads for Gambling. It is primarily concerned that the nation's game is being tarnished by betting. An Ipsos study, published only eight months after the launch of Ontario's iGaming market, found 63 percent of Canadians agreed limits were needed for the placement and volume of gambling ads. Those may be signs that the public thinks government has finally pushed too far, but the displeasure is focussed on advertising, not the explosion in gambling.

A Pew Research poll reports 43 percent of US adults say the legal status of sports betting in most of the country is bad for society. Yet a 2026 poll of Canadians found 66 percent think sports betting is "detrimental to society." And the advertising continues unabated, even after major sports betting scandals. Jontay Porter of the Toronto Raptors was banned by the NBA for life in 2024 after it was revealed that he gambled on Raptors games, disclosed confidential team information to sports bettors, and limited his own performance for betting purposes. The scandals are shocking, but they disappear from the news in a few days. The ads roll on.

The same is true of the massive amounts legally wagered by Canadians. "I was horrified by the fact that we were getting more revenue from Atlantic Lotto than we were getting from corporate business tax," says former Newfoundland and Labrador Premier Clyde Wells. "That didn't seem right." Yet this is the reality we live in: gambling is bigger business than big business itself.

In Ontario, gross gambling revenues totalled about $9.35 billion in 2024–25, or $705 per adult. This is nearly a third of the corporate tax revenue collected ($27.8 billion) across Ontario's entire economy. It's challenging to raise taxes with Canadians feeling squeezed by rising living costs and incomes that aren't keeping pace, but, for decades, gambling has been viewed as a backdoor method of taxation. On a per capita basis, legal gambling revenues are equivalent to residents paying hundreds of dollars more annually in taxes. But while this strategy props up treasuries, it's frequently at the expense of marginalized residents, including those with the lowest incomes and others who become addicted to gambling.

PART 3

THE DATA BLACK HOLE

I was part of the first generation to grow up in Canadian gambling's expansion era. When I was born in 1986, buying lotto and scratch tickets, playing bingo, and betting on horses were legal. By the time I attended elementary school, legalized gambling was in overdrive. Noisy video lottery terminals became government-regulated and were deployed by the thousands. People could wager on sports parlays, and casinos started dotting the landscape. This included my hometown of Sydney, Nova Scotia. By the time my family got a home computer, offshore online casinos and poker rooms operated outside the reach of Canadian regulators. Debates sparked over whether it was "right" for governments to regulate them.

More than two decades later, the question is mostly settled. Former classmates have children old enough to have come of age in today's far more expansive gambling wave. Increasingly, gambling has been normalized by heavy marketing campaigns and 24/7 smartphone access. Our primary influences to gamble or not were behaviours observed in our families, but today gambling is so visible in society through heavy advertising campaigns, dodgy influencer spon-con, and 24/7 smartphone access, that it is widely considered acceptable, if not "normal." But I've never been able to shake the idea that Sydney's casino might not have been a great idea. There has been little analysis published anywhere. The full impacts of the casino, and those like it are unknown, and not only in Nova Scotia. When I began digging into the story seven years ago, I found that reporting on the gambling industry in Canada was scarce.

I started reading Atlantic Canadian news articles, piecing together the public history of Nova Scotia's casinos. I looked for financial figures, milestone dates, government reports, opinion surveys, and the arguments of political players for and against the project. Occasionally, my research was punctuated by stories of gambling-related suicides. Some were local; others were from out of the region. Because they were spread out over time and across various print newspapers, they would have struck most readers as rare. But I was encountering gambling-related suicides in close succession. It was jarring. I felt saddened by the hopelessness and helplessness of the deceased, and uneasy with what appeared to be an obvious link between the increasing death toll and the expansion of legalized gambling in Canada.

I published a four-part investigation into Sydney's casino with the *Cape Breton Spectator*, touching briefly on gambling-related suicides. In 2017, a local psychotherapist had told the *Cape Breton Post* that he felt gambling addiction was a major cause of local suicides. When I spoke with him in 2020, he still believed there was a connection, but it was difficult to isolate gambling as a cause without a suicide note that explicitly mentioned it. Gambling addiction is a "comorbid" condition usually present alongside other medical or mental health disorders.

I asked the province's Medical Examiner Service for comment. A spokesperson said over email that the service's investigations provide only a person's identity and the cause and manner of their death. "Factors that may have contributed to the person's decision to [die by suicide] are either difficult or impossible to know and report reliably."

At the time, I knew too little about gambling-related suicides to push back. I concluded that section of my work by suggesting the province either "doesn't fully understand the extent of the addiction its casinos feed, or it simply turns a blind eye to the difficulties residents experience trying to access treatment." I wasn't aware that the answer might fall between those extremes.

Having finished my series, I wanted to write more about gambling-related suicides. I felt a duty, having read about these horrors, to keep asking questions. I also wanted to know what progress, if any, had been made on preventing gambling-related suicides. In 2022, I was awarded a Michener-Deacon investigative journalism fellowship to find out how many gambling-related suicides had occurred in Canada since 2000 and what, if anything, was happening to prevent them. I also wanted to know how these deaths shape decisions about gambling expansion and policy.

It seemed like a straightforward concept to investigate. All provincial coroners and medical examiners had shared some form of gambling-related suicide data with media, and in 2003, they announced they would record the deaths using a shared standard. Surely, if this information was collected, it should be easy to organize, track, and share.

Continued expansion of gambling in Canada made the subject timely. I was starting just before the launch of Ontario's privately run, government-regulated iGaming online casino market and the legalization of single-sports betting. There were other developments promising for my research, including peer-reviewed research linking gambling and suicides, and increasingly mainstream discussion of gambling's downsides elsewhere.

In Australia, thirty gambling industry and mental health stakeholders had released a report calling for the identification and recording of gambling-related suicides. Two academic reviews of data (one spanning thirteen years, the other eight) from Australia's Victoria state estimated, respectively, that gambling contributed to nearly 2 and 4 percent of suicides. "That's an undercount, but it's a start," said Angela Rintoul, a gambling and suicide researcher at the Melbourne School of Population and Global Health. She and her co-author, Charles Livingstone, suggest the actual figures in Victoria are higher because gambling-related suicides are often hidden, misclassified, or simply never identified.

The people who investigate suicides in Canada work primarily at the offices of the chief coroner and chief medical examiner, which exist in each province and territory. Coroner and medical examiner offices serve similar purposes, investigating deaths that appear to be unnatural, unexplained, sudden, or suspicious, and identifying the mortality trends that help us make sense of death in our society. But they rely on different systems, with policies and procedures that don't always overlap. The most significant difference is that coroners can sometimes be laypeople from a variety of backgrounds, while medical examiners must be trained doctors.

As part of their work, coroners and medical examiners investigate suicides. According to the medico-legal nonprofit Canadian Medical Protective Association, they "may identify practices or conditions that could have led to the death and may make recommendations to prevent similar deaths." Sometimes this means filling out routine reports, which may include contextual details from those close to the deceased or, if one of the few suicide deaths where a note is left behind, they may record stated factors. Rarely, these investigations are subject to a longer process commonly known as a coroner's inquest, which is like a small trial open to the public.

A chief coroner or medical examiner leads each office and generally has long-term experience in this corner of public service. They shape the office's strategic directions much like a CEO does at a company. While they are government-funded and often under the oversight of a province or territory's ministry of justice, the offices operate at arm's length from government. Coroner and medical examiner offices must follow statutes laid out in the province's coroner or medical examiners act, but they can choose their own standards in performing certain tasks—like how they record suicide risk factors in a deceased person's file.

Between 2001 and 2002, Nova Scotia's chief medical examiner's office asked about gambling every time a suicide happened. It was within the office's right. Then it stopped. No legislative changes were required, only the office's desire to end the protocol. That this sort of whim could affect the collection of suicide risk factor information was one of the earliest obstacles I encountered in my research. It compounded the already fraught challenge of figuring out how many gambling-related suicides occurred.

Suicides are widely believed to be undercounted in general. Research suggests more than 30 percent get missed by coroners or medical examiners. A 2017 *Canadian Medical Association Journal* (CMAJ) study attributed underreporting of suicides in Canada to several factors, including "disagreement amongst death investigators on burden of proof" and a "lack of national death reporting standards." That's to say nothing of judgement calls that may be unknowingly incorrect—accidental drug overdoses classified as intentional suicides or *vice versa.*

Reasons people die by suicide are often hard to track because the deceased can't speak for themselves. Dr. Matthew Bowes, Nova Scotia's chief medical examiner since 2006 says it's not always within his confidence level to say why someone lost their life to suicide. Legislation governing reporting means he and his peers don't have to—their mandate requires only certain basic info. "We're tasked with the how and what, and you're interested in the great why," he says. Sometimes he and his colleagues "*glimpse* the great why," but it is complex to assess.

I asked provinces for the annual figures of suicides where gambling was listed as a potential risk factor (in addition to the keywords casino, gamble, and VLT), for all years available up to the end of 2023. Ultimately, eight provincial coroner or medical examiner offices shared data with me, all except Newfoundland and Labrador and Prince Edward Island. Between the data they shared and other previously published information, this yielded a total of 965 recorded gambling-related suicide deaths between 2000 and 2023. Accordingly on average, one Canadian dies about every nine days from a gambling-related suicide.

The term "at least" is necessary, not only because there are years when zero have been formally recorded and others for which I have been unable to acquire data, but also because some gambling-related suicides are likely missed due to the normal challenges of recording suicide data.

While experts suggest gambling-related suicides make up at least 5 percent of overall suicide totals, no provincial average I received reached that level, even in provinces that provided full data sets, including British Columbia (84), Ontario (267), and Quebec (456). The average of recorded deaths across Canadian provinces amounts to about 1 percent of overall suicides.

The lowest recorded annual provincial gambling-related suicide totals I collected came from Manitoba and New Brunswick, where in some years no deaths were recorded. The highest total was 3.9 percent in Saskatchewan in 2001. That came thanks to a one-time release of data by the coroner's service to *The Globe and Mail.* The only data the Saskatchewan office shared with me was from 2015 to 2021 when the province ran a project tracking risk factors, including gambling. The coroner's service said in 2024 it hadn't tracked gambling as a suicide risk factor since completing the project.

In neighbouring Alberta, the medical examiner's office broke figures into multi-year groups, which made the prevalence rates appear to decline. I asked the office to break it down annually, but it refused, citing privacy concerns. I asked Halifax-based privacy lawyer David Fraser about this and was told the main concern with data is inadvertently identifying someone's personal information. For instance, if Alberta shared that there was one gambling-related suicide in a county that had one suicide that year, it could potentially identify the person. But there were enough suicides and few enough identifying factors that this shouldn't have affected my request.

Most provincial figures fell below 2.5 percent, and based on expert opinions and my research, the discrepancy between that number and what experts expect appears to owe less to provinces actually having significantly lower gambling-related suicide rates, but because the counting is so haphazard. This means all figures reviewed fall below the best estimates of researchers and the recorded coronial data in places like Victoria, Australia, and Hong Kong published in academic journals.

In one report, a Coroners Court of Victoria case investigator recorded "engaged in gambling" near time of death for 197 suicides during a thirteen-year period and noted that there was evidence of gambling in a further 193 cases but insufficient context to confirm it as a risk factor. Counting all the cases with insufficient context nearly doubles the prevalence to 8 percent. This suggests gambling deaths can make up a considerable portion of suicides, even before reforms that would collect better data on gambling as a suicide risk factor.

That none of the numbers I collected met or exceeded 5 percent in a single calendar year, which would have been a "plausible outcome," according to Angela Rintoul, seemed at odds with the continued expansion of gambling in Canada. It suggested a lack of investigative rigour. Rintoul adds that gambling-related suicides could potentially rise to 15 to 20 percent of the total if tracked using the broadest definition of gambling as a risk factor—for instance, that the person was an active gambler, but not necessarily addicted according to clinical definitions. A review of 2003 coronial data in Hong Kong found nearly 20 percent of suicides were gambling-related. Financial records are reviewed closely for debts, gambling behaviours, and insurance in unnatural deaths in Hong Kong, including suicides. In turn, news reports about suicide deaths in Hong Kong sometimes specify financial risk factors.

If Canadian provinces had robust reporting methods and recorded very low rates of gambling-related suicides, it would be easier to believe that Canada hasn't much of a problem. But tracking methods across the country are, at best, imprecise, and in two provinces, PEI and NL, the data hasn't yet been shared.

PEI had at least one gambling-related suicide on the public record during the period I was researching. It was reported in *The Globe* in 2009. Deputy chief coroner Dr. Brandon Webber told me in 2022 that he remembered working on one recent case that might have been gambling-related, although his office provided no formal recorded data.

In Newfoundland and Labrador, there have been multiple gambling-related deaths referenced in media, including Susan Piercey's in 2003. When I spoke with two of Newfoundland and Labrador's chief medical examiners, the retired chief examiner, Dr. Simon Avis, and his successor, Dr. Nash Denic, Avis said he likely worked on gambling-related suicide cases, but Denic didn't recall working on any. This may be, in part, because for many years Denic's caseload was about a third of Avis's. Denic recalled investigating suicides where "financial issues" were a risk factor and conceded that gambling could be one of those issues.

Little is known specifically about the connection between debt and suicide, but economic hardship is widely considered a suicide risk, including in India where a study using media articles on gambling-related suicides in India linked 83 percent of them to financial losses. Variants of the term "financial issues" or "financial problems" appeared frequently in my research, including in a paper about suicides in Newfoundland and Labrador co-authored by Dr. Avis. It found a "history of gambling" appeared as a precipitating factor in 2.2 percent of reviewed files, while financial problems appeared in 3.6 percent. Though both factors could appear together, it's possible some people's "financial problems," if interrogated deeper, might stem from gambling. In files from Quebec reviewed for this investigation, about 65 percent of gambling-related suicides featured debt or financial problems as a risk factor, with 37 percent of files containing the latter, less precise category.

When I mentioned that Dr. Denic's office could ask the question of what is meant by financial issues, he showed an openness. "Gambling could be one of the things that we don't ask the question for," he said. "Maybe it's something that we can change."

In 2024, his office hinted that he may have taken this to heart. "While the OCME does not currently track gambling as a risk factor for suicide, it is being explored as a factor to be captured during OCME investigations going forward," a representative wrote.

Progress, perhaps, but this came two decades after a promise was made (and broken) to collect gambling-suicide data and use it to keep people safe. Why was I effectively starting from scratch?

It's not as though the data problem had never been noticed before. On February 23, 2003, Canadian Press journalists Sue Bailey and Louise Elliott reported that gambling-related suicide numbers might be higher than previously stated, and that such deaths were unevenly tracked across Canada. Bailey and Elliott focused on establishing the number of deaths occurring in order to convince decision-makers and other stakeholders to take gambling-related suicide seriously. They built their investigation around previously unreleased data from the Alberta and Nova Scotia medical examiner's offices. They linked gambling to 10 percent of Albertan suicides in 2001 and 6 percent of Nova Scotian suicides over the prior two years. There had been little discussion of these deaths in a national context, in part because gambling falls in provincial rather than a federal jurisdiction.

The reporters relied on scattered figures that coroner and medical examiner offices had previously shared with media. The samples were small enough for critics to dismiss. The only widely cited Canadian gambling-related suicide statistic was attributed to the Canada Safety Council (CSC). It suggested two hundred annual gaming-related suicides nationally—a figure equivalent to about 5 percent of overall suicides. Lewis Smith, CSC's national projects manager, says the council couldn't find supporting data and removed the stat from its website in 2018. The Alberta and Nova Scotia figures nevertheless suggested a larger problem. "Gambling is a major cause of suicide," said one source, a Nova Scotian clinician and addictions specialist who requested anonymity. "The Alberta figure is probably much closer to what is really happening."

In the course of their reporting, Bailey and Elliott called attention to inconsistent standards across the country. Ontario, for instance, listed "problem betting only when it's an obvious primary cause of self-inflicted death." Accordingly, "Ontario has logged fewer gambling-related suicides than Alberta, Nova Scotia, or Quebec where links have been more thoroughly probed and reported."

The reports also suggested the link between gambling and suicide was escaping politicians. Alberta's gaming minister, Ron Stevens, told the reporters he hadn't heard of a gambling-suicide connection. "Alberta's gambling-treatment facilities tell a different story," Bailey and Elliott wrote. "They say the suggestion of such a link is nothing new to them." Suicide expert and psychologist Antoon Leenaars told the reporters: "We need much more in-depth study and much more open-mindedness at coroners' offices. [The numbers are] pointing out the risk is high. We need to understand this better."

More skeptical commenters didn't doubt a gambling-suicide link but disbelieved that it could be recorded. They argued that the multi-factor nature of suicide made attributing deaths to a "cause" such as gambling difficult. Dr. Avis in Newfoundland and Labrador said the numbers suggested gambling-related suicides were a topic worth studying but that it was challenging to be definitive about. "They can't say for sure gambling [caused] suicide; all they can say is the person who committed suicide gambled." This is correct on its face but sidesteps the issue by imposing an unrealistically narrow standard of proof.

That investigation inspired public debate across Canada in provincial legislatures and on radio talk shows. A Nova Scotia health ministry spokesperson said it would "support a national effort to establish better reporting on issues like problem gambling prevalence and suicide, 'so that you can compare across provinces.'" Chief coroners and medical examiners added gambling-related suicides to the agenda of a national meeting in Iqaluit later that year. The meeting's host, the Canadian Association for Suicide Prevention, says it has no details on file about the event, and that its meetings are merely occasions to exchange ideas. As Nova Scotia Chief Medical Examiner Dr. Matthew Bowes wrote in the CMAJ, "this forum has no budget or lawful mandate to set and enforce standards."

Dr. Avis attended the 2003 Iqaluit meeting, and his recollection is in line with his comments mentioned earlier: "Whilst we recognized your gambling might be a precipitating factor [in suicides], that is very difficult to really determine." He remembers no clear agreement among his peers over whether tracking gambling-related suicides was possible.

The hands-on approach that Nova Scotia had tried was already on the outs. It was unappealing to some health professionals to ask probing questions, in part because of the potentially low return of affirmative answers. A more passive option was present in Manitoba, where the chief medical examiner's office implemented a check box in or around 1999, which read "death was gambling related."

"The spirit behind it was for the data entry person to check this box if it was obvious from the investigation that gambling played a role in that person's life to commit suicide," says Gordon Holens, a long-time statistician at Manitoba's Office of the Chief Medical Examiner. "There was no formal definition attached to checking this box."

It worked as a data collection tool for a while—the office recorded seventeen gambling-related suicides from 2000 to the end of 2005. But in 2006, 2007, and 2008 the office recorded zero. Other nonconsecutive years with zero recorded gambling-related suicides followed.

Provinces like Quebec had been recording gambling in suicide investigations if family or friends mentioned it or the deceased wrote it in a suicide note, and this is how those assembled at the Iqaluit meeting agreed to record the data. Avis said coroner and medical examiner offices would record each case where "gambling was a potential or possible contributing stressor—implying something that tipped the person over the edge." His characterization suggests the decision was a compromise—a way to record the information without adding additional work, while also avoiding setting strict rules or new parameters that might prompt a backlash.

In the years since that meeting, a development mused about at the time has come into force. Bailey and Elliott reported that a new national database could soon assist with the recording of suicide risk factors like gambling. Now active for two decades, the Canadian Coroner Medical Examiner Database (CCMED) is a joint project of the thirteen provincial and territorial coroner and medical examiners offices, as well as Public Health Agency of Canada and Statistics Canada. It collects information from all thirteen offices, but because levels of detail are voluntary and differ, the CCMED does not recommend disaggregating data from the national level.

I wanted to see if CCMED might have more fulsome data than the provinces, so I asked for its gambling-related suicide records. In response, CCMED searched its database using the keywords casino, gamble, gambling and VLT, then manually reviewed narrative reports to remove non-gambling-related deaths. It found 250 in its database from 2006 to 2023 for provinces outside Quebec, 205 male and 45 female. About 75 percent of the gambling-related suicides showed evidence of problematic gambling, with the remainder featuring other evidence of gambling, gambling prior to death, or mentioning a family member with a gambling addiction.

Even with the full participation of provinces, the database yields about half the number of gambling-related suicides I collected by contacting individual provinces. CCMED acknowledges that its count may be underestimated.

The 2003 conversation on gambling-related suicides and the promise made by coroner and medical examiners to improve tracking put the ball in the court of public servants. Provincial legislatures and coroner and medical examiner offices were on notice to take direct action to combat the problem. But nothing of substance happened.

Harm reduction resources to help people with gambling problems went to public awareness campaigns and prevention programs. Data remained inconsistent and incomplete. No suicide records prompted provinces to adjust their gambling industry policies, either by halting expansion or proposing contraction in the future. The issue quietly fell off the agenda.

When the Canadian Association for Suicide Prevention created a draft national suicide strategy in 2004, it didn't mention gambling. The same was true of its update five years later.

In 2005, a report on gambling was submitted to the Law Commission of Canada, part of a project that commissioned expert reports on several different areas of society under the theme "what is a crime?"

"In terms of suicide, it's evident that some of these tragic outcomes are related to a gambling problem," write authors Colin Campbell of Douglas College and Timothy Hartnagel and Garry Smith of the University of Alberta. Yet the prevalence of such deaths is "unclear" and "it's not easy to attribute the suicide entirely to a gambling problem." To make their point, they referred to suicide figures from Edmonton. Three of ninety-five suicides in 2001, or just over 3 percent, were marked as gambling-related because of what was indicated in suicide notes. Following the 2003 announcement to record gambling-related suicides and considering the general practices of Canadian coroners and medical examiners today, we would count gambling as a risk factor in these deaths. But the authors expressed doubt, writing "it's unclear whether there were other underlying disorders or related circumstances that at least partially caused these tragedies."

This line of thinking only holds if gambling's role in suicide is black and white: a definitive "cause" or nothing. If a goal of recording risk factors is to use them to shape policy and prevention, it's less important whether or not gambling is the dominant reason someone dies by suicide. What matters is using its presence as a risk factor to get gamblers critical, timely help to prevent unnecessary deaths.

The authors also question the standard applied to suicide notes. Do we accept what's written as an objective truth because it is how the suicidal person views their situation? Or do we view it as subjective, influenced by other factors that may be beyond their control? For example, if someone writes a suicide note that mentions gambling as the cause of their death, but they also live with other risk factors such as alcoholism and lifelong depression, do those health issues supersede the deceased's convictions?

These same questions were addressed in *A Protocol for Determining Gambling-Related Suicides in Psychological Autopsy Studies*, published in 2003 in the *Gaming Law Review* by the University of Sydney's Alexander Blaszczynski and Christian Marfels of Dalhousie University. The authors outline the different sources of information that could link gambling to a suicide and produced a scoring rubric. While they accept a person's self-identification as a gambler in a suicide note, they later suggest that once it's established someone is a gambler, it becomes necessary to exclude some cases. For Blaszczynski and Marfels this includes "where there is evidence of a chronic history of psychiatric illness such as schizophrenia or major depression that predates the onset of gambling behaviour, personality disorder known to be associated with elevated risk for self-harm such as borderline personality disorder, interpersonal problems characterized by a chronic history of social isolation and withdrawal from early childhood, evidence of childhood history of sexual or physical abuse and chronic substance abuse, the onset of which clearly emerges prior to gambling."

If the above were applied as the standard, it could negate how people perceive their own or others' experiences with gambling, and a large number of cases across Canada and other nations might not count as gambling-related suicides. Angela Rintoul says this concept coloured discussion among her peers for years. In a 2025 paper, she writes that the article doesn't provide evidence for its assertions and ignores that gambling can be a dominant factor in a suicide. She adds that the lead author "now discloses extensive gambling operator funding," although he didn't at the time of the article.

One conclusion of the Law Commission of Canada study by Campbell et al. was that Ottawa needed to launch a "long overdue" inquiry into Canada's gambling industry, given a "failure to consider the long-term impact on public welfare."

"We'd like to get to the bottom of this $13-billion industry," co-author Smith later told *The Globe*. "What's it doing to us?"

Commissions of inquiry are established by the federal cabinet "to fully and impartially investigate issues of national importance." According to a list of these commissions, dating back to 1868 on the federal government's website, gambling has never been covered.

A definitive signal that coroner and medical examiner progress on gambling-related suicides was a mirage would arrive in a 2007 article in *The Tyee* about the "broken promise on gambling suicides." Written by Tom Barrett, it reported that British Columbia still hadn't started tracking gambling-related suicides, even after a high-profile murder-suicide that involved gambling. Barrett also wrote that Nova Scotia had "quietly stopped collecting data in the summer of 2004," although he doesn't specify if that means they stopped asking for it, or recording it entirely.

A study released a few months after the *Tyee* article in a September 2007 issue of *The Canadian Journal of Psychiatry* found "an association between gambling, when taken to excess, and self-harm." Although the study didn't establish a causal relationship between gambling and suicide, it found that over their lifetimes people with gambling problems were several times more likely to attempt suicide than average Canadians. The authors suggested that in the future, "respondents with a history of attempted suicide should be asked whether problems related to gambling precipitated the episode of self-harm." They went on to add that "despite the lack of a clear causal relation, this finding is of public health concern." Another warning that went unheeded.

* * *

Coroners and medical examiners have a valid point when they argue that the causes of suicide are complex. In the *Tyee* article and others, gambling is framed as a "cause" of suicide, or even the "main cause" of suicide. While people may casually discuss suicides this way, it is not scientifically accurate.

When we learn someone has died by suicide, our minds should not immediately jump to a single reason. They should hold space for the multiple factors that may have played roles in a person's decision to die. It is more accurate to present suicide as a risk factor than a cause. Accepting this point is helpful in discussing the issue with people and experts who will otherwise use semantics to deny the existence of a problem.

Even when careful wording is employed, pushback still happens. An Alberta Justice spokesperson called me to explain why my questions were faulty, yet requests with the exact same wording were easily understood by other provinces who shared the data I wanted without complaint. Alberta Justice didn't stop there. In 2003, it was reported that the prior year, Alberta listed gambling "in the files of 48 suicides out of 418 counted so far; in 2001, in 46 of 482 cases; and in 2000, in 54 of 430 suicides." Yet the province's medical examiner office told me a relatively modest twenty-seven such deaths occurred between 2000 and 2004 and refused to break them down by year. Alberta Justice said it "is not possible for the current Office of the Chief Medical Examiner staff to comment on the parameters that OCME staff used in 2003." A representative further argued that for the 2003 article medical investigators were recording "gambling on the file of any suicide victim if a relative or friend mentions it or if there's evidence of gambling at the scene of death." My request was for "the number of suicides where gambling was noted as a risk factor." In their view, these two requests were separate questions. But if gambling is recorded in the file, how is it not a risk factor?

The defensive approach of Alberta Justice is, unfortunately, typical. Rather than admit that figures differ radically and illogically, that recordkeeping is poor, and that the issue of gambling-related suicides is frequently overlooked, the government suggests that the question, if not the entire line of inquiry, is faulty. If activists, journalists, and other non-experts are not always precise in discussions of gambling-related suicides, they are at least asking their questions in good faith. It is difficult to say the same for officials who bury or obscure data and use semantics to avoid an important public health conversation. Coroner and medical examiner offices and government employees should be steering discussions toward gambling's role as a risk factor, instead of dismissing it.

In 2009, *The Globe* published an investigation on gambling in Canada, including statistics on gambling-related suicides provided by provincial coroner and medical examiner offices. This was nearly six and a half years after the supposed standardization in tracking gambling-related suicide data. "Not all provinces track such suicides and those that do, track them in slightly different ways," *The Globe* said. All provinces except Nova Scotia shared figures with *The Globe*, for a total of 420 suicides, but the data were inconsistent and difficult to compare. Two provinces offered cumulative figures only, while others shared them broken down annually. New Brunswick expressed part of their data in fiscal years making it unclear how many suicides happened each calendar year prior to 2005. British Columbia told *The Globe* that nineteen deaths had taken place between 2003 and 2008, notably different from *The Tyee* article two years earlier. Also, if the province hadn't started tracking the suicides by 2007, how were they now sharing earlier data?

The Globe reported Newfoundland and Labrador identifying "nine deaths from Jan. 1, 1997, to Dec. 31, 2008, in which gambling was thought to be a stressor." Since the province shared no data with me, I could not confirm the figure. "[T]he statistics would have most likely been collected through a manual file review for the time period in question," the office said over email. The most notable trend in all this is that some coroner and medical examiners approach gambling-related suicides differently each time the question is asked.

According to *The Globe*, Nova Scotia did "not track the cause of suicides as it says there is no way to gather the information." In less than a decade, Nova Scotia had gone from being at the forefront of tracking gambling-related suicides in Canada to publicly suggesting it was impossible.

Two years later, Nova Scotia's strained viewpoint again made national news. A major study on gambling's economic and social impacts was attempted by University of Alberta economist Mark Anielski. He was the lead author of a new framework he hoped would revolutionize evaluating the socio-economic impact of gambling (SEIG for short) in Canada. He premiered the framework in a 2008 paper, which referred to a search for a "gold standard" understanding of gambling's effects. This search required, in his view, examining effects on everyone from individual gamblers on up to the provinces themselves through a series of cost-benefit analyses. These would be conducted under six "impact themes" including health and well-being, which counted suicide among the potential costs.

The SEIG framework had limitations. American economics professor and gambling scholar Douglas Walker underscores the challenge of attributing the costs of certain social offshoots to gambling. It's difficult to do with any framework, not just SEIG. "How should we handle a problem gambler who is also a drug addict, for example, and causes $5,000 worth of social costs?" Walker wrote. "What proportion of the cost should be attributed to problem gambling, and what proportion to drug use? Most studies in the gambling literature simply attribute the entire cost to problem gambling, certainly overstating the social costs of gambling."

The SEIG framework tried to address this challenge through detailed cost-benefit analysis. These included taking the type of gambling into account when assigning impacts, rather than generic gambling. Anielski wrote, for instance, that slot machines and VLTs "may have greater deleterious effects than playing bingo or buying lottery tickets." As well, the framework acknowledged that different groups from non-gamblers through gamblers of various risk levels faced different "costs."

Nova Scotia was the guinea pig for applying the SEIG framework to the real world and establishing an "analytical, factual and objective" baseline for gambling's social and economic impacts. The province had commissioned the study as part of its *A Better Balance* gambling strategy, but cancelled it after reading the first draft. In 2010, Anielski wrote in a blog post that he had been accused of "using faulty research methods and flawed statistics, and of focusing too narrowly on the well-being impacts of a relatively few number of Nova Scotia's problem gamblers and on video lottery terminals (VLTs)."

Despite the province calling the data flawed, The Canadian Press and GameOver VLTs appealed to the Information and Privacy Commissioner, arguing the report still merited release, whatever the methodology. The public could make its own judgement. It was published online in 2011.

Nearly five hundred pages long with its appendices, the SEIG study features hundreds of annotations from the province in foreboding red text, which it wrote are "neither meant to be critical nor corrective, but rather are meant to draw attention to possible concerns." Among them was that some information and statistics used in the report fell outside the study's 2001–2007 time frame, that "inconsistent" inclusion and exclusion of statistics related to First Nations gambling was "problematic," and that Anielski sometimes analyzed and drew conclusions despite acknowledging "that conclusions cannot be made as there is not enough information available, sample sizes are too small, or significant difference does not exist." Instead of allowing Anielski to address the large number of criticisms and fixes it identified, the province cancelled the study.

The most controversial impact reviewed was Anielski's estimations of gambling-related suicides. Citing the 2003 Canadian Press report and a health department official, he estimated 6 percent of all Nova Scotia suicides might be gambling-related. The government denied the health department official shared such an estimate, although Anielski referenced the person by name in his source list. I filed a freedom of information request for their correspondence but was told no record existed.

The search for the gold standard ended. Anielski dropped the SEIG idea and pivoted his research toward the economics of "well-being." Nobody else built upon his vision in the years since. A few days after responding to my information request, the government quietly removed Anielski's report from its website. That is the reality of government data in the new gambling age.

PART 4

HIDDEN CONSEQUENCES

On September 18, 2009, Chris Parlow bet his last $18 on the New York Yankees beating the Seattle Mariners. He listened to the game on his car radio in a remote wooded area in northern Ontario, about a day's drive from The Pas, Manitoba, where he was living. He was out of gas and alone.

Parlow told loved ones he was taking a fishing trip, but left Manitoba in his grey Ford Fusion with intentions of visiting his birthplace in New Brunswick, where he planned to die by suicide.

He didn't know that there was a missing person's alert out for him, with his family, friends, and coworkers concerned by his absence over the past several days. Unlike an alert nearly a dozen years earlier that mentioned a missing Manitoba man was a gambler, this one said nothing of the sort. For two decades, Parlow had kept his gambling addiction secret and he wasn't confiding in medical professionals or his loved ones. "Nobody had any idea that I was who I was, a gambling addict who was out of control."

Over the years, every dollar he could muster fuelled his addiction. Parlow lost his house and cars. He filed for bankruptcy.

A police officer, tipped by hunters to a strange car parked in the woods, found Parlow that night. "For the first time in my life, I told somebody the truth," he says. The officer took Parlow to a hospital. Upon returning to Manitoba, he entered a treatment facility. Tragedy was averted.

As Parlow worked on his recovery, he spoke out about gambling addiction and how it led him to consider ending his life. When Casinos of Winnipeg announced a pilot project for round-the-clock opening hours, he shared his story with CBC Manitoba, suggesting the move would only create more hardships like his. "What often happens at the end of all the chaos is we decide to take our life because we just can't take it anymore," he said.

Parlow, who now lives in British Columbia, hasn't placed a bet since that fateful night in 2009. He pursues passions like photographing wildlife or enjoying his season tickets for the BC Lions, where he once would have spent his time and money chasing bets. He frequently takes his camera to BC Place, not just to capture shots of the game. "My camera is kind of like a buffer between me and all the [gambling] ads," he says.

In Parlow's view, there's a deeper reason coroners and medical examiners should watch for these deaths beyond their capacity to help. "Covering up or not acknowledging the suicides is perpetuating secrets and perpetuating an illness that avoids detection at all costs," he says. It reminds him of the years he kept his gambling addiction secret. "We don't need people like medical examiners to be complicit with us."

Parlow is an example of someone who was reached in time. Stories like his, of gambling-driven suicidal thoughts and attempts, are as under-discussed as suicide deaths. One review of over thirteen studies found the range for suicide attempts and thoughts among gamblers surveyed went as high as 40 percent and 81 percent, respectively. Sometimes these figures get dismissed because they may refer to "lifetime" suicidal ideation, which could happen before the onset of gambling problems. But prior suicide attempts put people at greater risk of attempting it again, with or without the presence of gambling. Rather than being discounted, the presence of gambling in these instances needs to be taken more seriously.

It's no wonder there's silence. When people share their stories of challenging experiences, they put themselves at risk of misunderstanding, public judgment, and stigma. For all the progress that has been made in discussing mental health, there is still stigma surrounding suicides.

Researcher Leigh Huggard says mental illnesses considered controllable and deterministic (such as attributed to childhood upbringing) face the most stigma. Those viewed as uncontrollable or temporary are viewed with less stigma. "Based on this, I would expect that gambling as a root cause would be associated with some stigma, because it might be viewed as being within a person's control," she says. Though some people may view it as "somewhat deterministic" that some people may be naturally susceptible to gambling addiction, she adds, "I would expect it to be associated with some stigma, since it is unlikely to be perceived as both temporary and uncontrollable."

Andrew, a gambler in recovery, thinks part of the reason gambling-related suicides don't get discussed is that gambling isn't as visible a problem as other addictions can be. "No one can tell you have a problem, until there's a problem," he says. "Either you've committed a crime or you've committed suicide."

Andrew (not his real name) says suicide was a lingering thought for years throughout his addiction. He would gamble late into the night and was constantly anxious about having stolen a five-figure sum from his employer. "In my case, I don't think it would have culminated into considering suicide without gambling," he says.

There was a day Andrew was ready to take his life. He reached out for help instead. He tried calling his girlfriend and his mother, but couldn't reach either. He ended up asking his employer to meet. Over coffee, he came clean about the theft and his addiction. "The minute I actually committed to telling someone, that's kind of when the suicidal thoughts—that was the worst of it, I guess—all went away," Andrew says.

Dr. Matthew Bowes, Nova Scotia's chief medical examiner, thinks we should prioritize the tracking of suicidal attempts and thoughts over suicide deaths. They are easier to quantify and can have an impact on broader healthcare systems, for instance, if people in gambling-related distress show up at already resource-scarce emergency rooms. Further, the only way to stop gambling-related suicides from happening is to intervene early.

Despite this, no website of a major mental health or suicide prevention organization lists gambling-related suicide as its own category. It also isn't currently part of publicly funded suicide prevention programming in any province. This seems to be a dangerous oversight with about a million Canadians at risk for gambling addiction.

Another gambler in recovery, Gail, says that after admitting her addiction to her family, her spouse asked to separate. Faced with the dissolution of her marriage and a half-million-dollar debt, she considered suicide. One factor that dissuaded her was witnessing the impact of a neighbour's suicide on their family and friends. For the last fifty-plus years, it's been commonly cited that one suicide affects six people; recent figures suggest that 135 people are affected to varying degrees.

"I don't know if I have another run through the gambling mill in me," Gail says, and she's made life changes to help her focus on abstaining. This includes handing control of her finances to her new partner to avoid potential temptation. But she enjoys her life in recovery, which includes giving back to others as a certified peer gambling counsellor. She's noticed some people return to gambling and end up worse off than during previous lows. "I'm not going to do worse off, because worse off to me means dead," she says.

* * *

A widely held, neoliberal view is that gambling is a personal choice. People who do it compulsively simply exercise that freedom to a greater extent than others. But a gambling disorder is not a "personal choice," or departure from a "good" moral path. It is an illness recognized in the latest edition of the *Diagnostic and Statistical Manual of Mental Disorders* (DSM-5). And the personal-choice view neglects that in Canada many gambling ventures are owned by government, not private enterprise. Canadians expect governments to have a different duty of care and harm reduction, rather than profit from game design and marketing techniques that help people to gamble more compulsively.

By the time casual players become addicted to gambling, they face an array of consequences that affect their health, emotional stability, relationships, and finances. Every addicted gambler will experience the challenges of addiction differently, but an important commonality that has emerged over time is that their gambling addiction puts them at a higher risk to feel suicidal.

Though gambling addiction can be a leading suicide risk factor, it is widely acknowledged to compound effects of other suicide triggers like anxiety, depression, or substance misuse. They can encourage each other like a pair of bad-influence friends. Someone who has anxiety and a gambling addiction might become more anxious as they watch their bank balance dwindle from betting losses. Someone who misuses alcohol might drink more to distract themselves from the relationship troubles their gambling creates.

Finnish researchers, in a review of twenty papers on gambling and suicide, specifically link indebtedness and shame caused by gambling as "an important contributor to suicide." Researchers from neighbouring Norway reported, after reviewing 107 papers, that suicide attempts, thoughts, and deaths among gamblers outpace the general population.

Some causes of and risk factors for gambling addiction outlined by Canada's largest mental health teaching hospital include easy gambling access, early big wins, and "mistaken beliefs about the odds of winning." All of these are increasingly present in our domestic gambling industry, particularly with the glut of advertising, which makes betting look fun, inconsequential, and lucrative. By regulating private online casinos and sportsbooks through regulated iGaming, as has happened in Ontario and Alberta, commercial companies previously consigned to the margins can now spend huge advertising budgets to fight for market share. This means offering deposit bonuses, free play, and other enticements to lure players to set up accounts and start playing. As part of the arrangement, companies have to follow steps like securing and maintaining RG Check accreditation. This requires meeting nine standards and forty-eight criteria that include having corporate policies for responsible gambling, maintaining self-exclusion programs, and taking steps to detect and prevent underage gambling. This implies a high duty of care on the part of operators, but it's a minimum. And stories have leaked that suggest these private operators do their best to keep big spenders gambling, even when they try to stop.

A November 2022 *Toronto Star* story, released several months after the launch of iGaming Ontario, included comments from insiders about how companies approach big spenders who want to stop wagering. "The insider said some VIP employees at the two operators are informally encouraged to do everything in their power to retain customers, including taking steps to dissuade high-spending players, internally referred to as 'degenerates,' from using responsible gambling tools to bar themselves from a company's online sites and apps—also known as self-excluding," writes Christine Dobby.

Running an iGaming industry requires trust and a good-faith partnership between private enterprise and government, but when enterprises are calling citizens "degenerates" and trying to elide the rules, it's not only distasteful, but predatory.

In *Everybody Loses*, Danny Funt writes that 2 or 3 percent of VIP sports gamblers can account for upwards of 60 percent of revenue. It would be reasonable to expect that government-owned gambling outlets, whether in-person or online, have similar outlier players whom they want to keep returning. July 2002 records from the Nova Scotia Gaming Corporation audit committee traced the cause for a decline in high-end slot play that year partly to a single player slowing down. "Player 1" was reported as having "coin-in" that declined from $12 million in 2000, to $6.6 million in 2001 to $225,000 for the first half of 2002. "The decline in play for this particular player, and other high-end players has had a significant impact on casino revenues." There have no doubt been multiple "Player 1s" across the nation, whose stories we'll never know.

This isn't charitable gaming. It's big business. Companies (and governments) behave this way because the industry doesn't make its gargantuan profits from casual players. Academic research frequently puts revenues from those addicted to gambling between 15 and 50 percent of the total depending on jurisdiction and time period. Nova Scotia is among the jurisdictions that has cemented this truth in the public record. A 2007 report commissioned by the province found 39.2 percent of gambling expenditures came from just 6.1 percent of the population at risk for gambling addiction. Six years later, Nova Scotia reported that "at risk" and "problem" gamblers contributed 42 percent of provincial gambling revenues. Even contrary-minded researchers put figures between 5 and 15 percent.

One Ontario gambler in recovery, Meghan, knew someone from a recovery group who self-excluded from an online casino because he wanted to stop gambling. "Within two minutes of him self-excluding that online casino gave him $2,000 in bonus funds and said, if you want to change your mind, here you go," she says. "That's pretty much going out to an AA meeting with a beer cart and being like, 'hey, alcoholics, do you want to have a drink right after your meeting?'"

Meghan, who estimates she gambled away $200,000 over the years, was a VIP who spent enough at her favourite online casino that it assigned her a staff member to share bonus offers, including events where she could hobnob with sports stars.

"I never actually went to those things, because part of me knew I would essentially be in a room with problematic gamblers because of the amount of money that we were dropping," she said.

Funt has written about VIP bettors being offered chances to throw out first pitches at Major League Baseball games, play pickup on NBA courts, or get flown to golf championships by helicopter, landing on the course. Funt says he has been trying, to no avail, to uncover the New Jersey VIP sports bettor who lost more than $100 million, and upon switching companies caused a "huge swing in market share." He also describes companies trying to portray themselves not as gambling firms, but friends. He learned that a VIP host at FanDuel sent a player a gift bag after his dog passed away; it included a blanket with the dog's photo printed on it. "So if you ever thought about dialing back your betting, know you're going to lose all these perks and you're going to lose a friend," Funt said in a panel discussion on consumer behaviour and guardrails for the sports betting industry. "That, I think, speaks to what an ethically fraught side of the business it is, because they're doing so many clever things to egg on people who are betting at a terrifying pace and a terrifying amount of money."

Gambling-addicted clients are increasingly present at the offices of Canadian bankruptcy and insolvency trustees. Since the introduction of iGaming in Ontario, gambling-related bankruptcies have quadrupled in the province. "Ten years ago I didn't see anyone, because you'd actually have to go into a casino," licensed insolvency trustee Rob Kilner told The Canadian Press in 2025. "It's just the last two, three years." Kilner says he has clients whose gambling debts range from a few thousand dollars to more than $250,000. This negatively affects the finances and credit of the gambler and their household for years, but also has wider economic spinoffs. The debts owed to various creditors don't vanish into the ether; the funds instead line the coffers of gambling enterprises and government.

While governments put out clear financial statements on their own revenues and losses, it's more fraught to track these levels for gamblers. The true scale of losses may remain unknown until it's too late.

* * *

After John Hallett's death, his daughter Karlene Baert went through his paperwork. Among the files, she found a letter to his bank, written in capital letters on lined paper as his losses mounted. He requested a loan and openly discussed his descent into gambling addiction, mentioning his wife's passing as the impetus. "Her death hit me hard and I felt I had nothing to live for," he wrote. "Soon as the loneliness got to me, I started to visit the casino. I was soon addicted and could not break the habit."

The concept of legacy debts or legacy harms apply to those who are in recovery from gambling, or die by gambling-related suicide. They can last for years, or affect multiple generations. Sometimes it's consumer debt accrued, such as a mortgage that survivors must pay off. But it could also result in a surviving spouse facing old age with a depleted retirement account, or a loved one never being paid back large personal loans.

Someone in recovery from gambling who loses their job due to their addiction might not ever reclaim previous heights of professional or income status. Bankruptcies and divorces can also cause financial ripple effects. Other gambling harms, write Matthew Rockloff et al., include reduced parental involvement in the lives of young children, which creates insurmountable deficits to "their developmental outcomes, including school performance, job prospects and lifetime potential."

In Baert's case, she was able to sell Hallett's house and settle the debts he left behind. Given how hard Hallett worked to save money all his life, Baert muses there should have been something to pass on. "There really was nothing left."

On Wednesday, September 7, 2005, family and friends gathered for Hallett's funeral service. Baert learned afterward that a casino employee was among the mourners. Another casino employee who attended Baert's church quit his job after he heard about Hallett's suicide. "He could no longer be a part of something that would cause that," she says.

Baert misses her father's energetic presence in her life. He fixed his own cars and did his own home repairs. He once tore up his back lawn to level it because he didn't like the way the lawnmower rolled across it. She remembers Hallett drilling cracked bricks out of the side of the house, one drill hole at a time, to the astonishment of his neighbours. "But that was just Dad," Baert says, "if he was going to do it he'd put his all into it."

She believes he would still be alive today, in his nineties, if it hadn't been for his gambling addiction.

"He had everything to live for."

* * *

The most recent in-depth investigation in Canada, prior to mine, was in Quebec. Unlike elsewhere in Canada, coroner investigation reports are considered public documents in Quebec and are available to anyone who requests them. *La Presse* identified 401 gambling-related suicides in Quebec's coronial files from 1993 (the year Montreal's casino opened and VLTs were launched) to 2018, after applying filters such as gambling mentioned in a family interview or suicide letter. Neither the province's ministry of health and social services nor the coroner's office could identify specific reforms after publication of the investigation.

I repeated the search, but updated the end date. If reading about suicides in the news was shocking, reading the forms themselves was overwhelming. That the details are tragic is a given. But a majority of these individuals faced challenges besides gambling. These included different combinations of alcoholism, drug problems, trouble with the law, mental health issues—ranging from anxiety to schizophrenia—divorces or breakups, homelessness, and job losses. In the absence of a letter stating why they're suicidal—reported in only a quarter of Quebec's cases according to my analysis—or mentioning it to family, it can be difficult to tell if any one is the cause. But when viewed together, there can be little doubt that gambling is a risk factor for dying by suicide, including as a primary factor.

With the help of research assistants, I manually reviewed files, keeping tabs on information such as age, gender, and whether suicide notes, divorces or breakups, presence of mental illness, and the catch-all term "financial problems" were mentioned.

Other groups considered at high risk for suicide often display identifiable characteristics that can help direct targeted interventions. Men, for instance, can be identified by gender, while youth and seniors can be identified by age. Indigenous people belong to a distinct population group, while LGBTQ individuals may self-identify as part of another. Quebec's suicide investigation files suggest that some of these same markers may also help identify gamblers at elevated risk of suicide. For instance, a man between the ages of fifty and sixty-five who gambles, faces financial problems, is divorced or separated, and misuses alcohol or drugs may be at elevated risk of gambling-related suicide, according to cases documented by coroners. Many of these characteristics are already common among people who die by suicide. The distinguishing factor is gambling, and these files suggest that recognizing it as a key risk factor may, in some cases, create opportunities for intervention that could save lives.

This isn't guesswork. Years of recorded data support such a conclusion. For instance, 86 percent of the gambling-related suicides in Quebec were male and one in five had divorced or separated. About 40 percent of the reports use the term pathological gambling and about half have debt or financial issues. For a majority of those who died, it was not their first suicide attempt. With knowledge like this, it's possible to take action. Primary care providers can recognize risk in their patients. Suicide prevention nonprofits can design resources that can successfully transfer life-saving messages to people at risk. Potential exists for each province to go through suicide investigations and identify the profiles of those at risk for gambling-related suicides, and from other suicide risk factors by looking for common themes in the recorded data.

The Quebec files also showed some of the variations that happen through personal interpretation by investigators. In some cases, this obscures gambling-related suicides by downplaying the role of gambling or not asking enough questions to draw firm connections.

In one coroner's report, the deceased is described as having lost his marriage to gambling and the coroner specifically writes that his suicide was precipitated by the loss of the marriage. But if gambling caused the divorce, then a root cause of the suicide should be gambling.

In another case, the only mention of gambling is the casino chip found in the deceased's pocket after death. It is possible that this person might have gone to a casino, lost money, and died that night by suicide. But there isn't enough information recorded to know. The deceased could have found the chip cleaning out a cupboard, or it might have been a lucky talisman. Even applying a low burden of proof—say, on the balance of the evidence versus beyond reasonable doubt—the chip's presence can't comfortably be ascribed to gambling problems without more information. If, in this instance, the coroner asked further questions about gambling, the answers are not recorded, which means we're left with few clues to find meaning.

* * *

While gamblers are often viewed as a monolith, it's more accurate to think about them as we do people who commit suicide. Gamblers, too, are a large group made up of smaller subgroups. Middle-aged men appear to be at a greater risk of gambling-related suicide than other players, and may be the dominant group, but others are vulnerable, too.

In this new era of gambling, numerous swaths of the population face heightened levels of risk from the allure of the casino in their pocket, and the pressure of advertising. Older Canadians have frequently been a target market for the gambling industry because they are believed to have time and money to burn. Yet some have limited earning capacity. While only 6 percent of Canadian elders are considered low-income, the third of them who pay rent or a mortgage struggle with their bills. This imperils their finances in a unique way. One woman from Victoria, BC, developed dementia in her eighties, lost nearly $300,000 in gambling at a local casino, and filed for bankruptcy.

As one study puts it, older gamblers "have less time and fewer financial resources to recover from social, financial and, particularly, the medical and psychiatric consequences resulting from disordered gambling." Yet it's easier to attract older gamblers than ever before.

One academic review found that gambling among the elderly is encouraged by several factors present in Canada: industry expansion, marketing campaigns, and availability and accessibility. In the United States, which has experienced a similar betting boom, one therapist wrote in *The Guardian* that her "grandparent gambler base has exploded since 2018," following the legalization of sports betting in some states.

Alarms are also being raised about young gamblers, and not just freshly minted, age-of-majority youth. CAMH mentions on its website that research on young gamblers includes subjects as young as ten. Kids today are surrounded by gambling ads, accustomed to the dopamine hits from social media and even gambling-style play in popular video games. They are uniquely primed to become gamblers in ways past generations aren't. Despite the efforts to keep youth out of government-regulated gaming, age controls haven't made it to the black and grey markets.

A recent report on youth aged eighteen to twenty-nine who gambled online in the past year found nearly 25 percent "reported experiencing a high level of gambling-related harms, including reduction of savings, increased credit card debt and compromised well-being due to feelings of regret and self-perceived failure." Concerns arise because online gambling is more popular among youth (about one in three gamble online), but compared to gamblers who only play lotteries, online gamblers are more than twenty times more likely to report high gambling-related harm levels and more than forty-five times more likely to meet problem gambling criteria.

Young men are particularly at risk. "The introduction of online gambling and subsequent privatization with single-event sports betting were each associated with substantial increases in gambling-related helpline contacts, specifically in adolescent boys and young men, suggesting increased gambling problems, care-seeking, or both," write University of Toronto researchers in the CMAJ. They found that contacts to the ConnexOntario mental health and addictions hotline for gambling increased by 144 percent among Ontario males aged fifteen to twenty-four years compared to before the iGaming industry's launch, and 337.8 percent more than with no regulated online gambling at all, including PlayOLG.

Steve has been in recovery since 2019. "There's a difference between abstinence and recovery," he says. Previously he only focused on abstinence from gambling, which he saw as time off. Now he's actively in recovery, which for him involves following a twelve-step program and doing service work, including as an executive with Alberta Gamblers Anonymous. He knows what will happen if he veers off course. "I won't stop until I lose all my money. I'm going to be a liar. I'm going to be a thief," he says. "I might as well say bye-bye to my family and my friends and my work."

Gambling is more dangerous for youth because they are too young to truly understand what's at stake when their bets get out of hand, Steve says. "There's no information on how you could lose your life savings. You could lose your family, your wife might divorce you, your car will get taken away. These kids don't know the consequences, because they haven't had the experience yet."

Meghan grew up in Ontario as it underwent the wave of casino building that normalized and destigmatized gambling culture. Her son is growing up in the current era. She considers him "lucky" because of what she's been through. "I know how to teach him," she said of gambling addiction. "I know how to have those conversations."

But Meghan is less confident when it comes to the broader dialogues about gambling needed in today's society. "We don't know how to handle it."

PART 5

A PATH FORWARD

In his mid-teens, Jack Ritchie of Sheffield, England, started playing slot machines, hoping to win enough to buy "free" lunches. His new habit seemed innocent enough to start. But in the years that followed, Jack gambled away his bank overdraft, an inheritance, and his student loan.

By 2017, he was teaching English abroad in Hanoi, Vietnam. While this meant ditching many everyday routines from back home, his gambling habit continued online. Jack died by suicide at age twenty-four, mentioning his gambling addiction in the note he left for his parents, Charles and Liz.

The Ritchies knew Jack struggled with gambling, but weren't aware of its connection with heightened suicide risks. "As far as we were aware, we were the first gambling suicide that had ever been," Charles Ritchie says.

Gambling is a bigger beast in the United Kingdom than in Canada. The nation offers similar ways to bet, including VLT-like fruit machines in pubs and online sports betting, but its gambling culture is on steroids. The United Kingdom is one of the world's most open online gambling markets and residents have dealt with barrages of marketing and promotions for many more years than Canadians have. Prior to a voluntary ban on front-of-shirt logo sponsorships took effect, one analysis suggested betting company logos appeared up to 3,500 times in the nation's beloved Premier League soccer matches. Another reports that about 70 percent of youth aged eleven to seventeen recall hearing or seeing gambling ads.

Following Jack's death, the Ritchies asked for a meeting with the chief executive officer of one of their son's most frequented gambling sites, William Hill. The firm had previously told media that it, and the whole industry, fell short in tackling gambling problems. The Ritchies thought the company might be receptive to Jack's story. Liz later wrote in *The Guardian* that in a meeting with the company's director of sustainability, the Ritchies' "calls for further measures were dismissed. Soon after we were escorted out of the building, quickly and rudely."

The couple decided to take action and started searching out news stories and contacting coroners and bereavement support networks to see how many other families had been bereaved by gambling-related suicides. Eventually, they compiled a list of more than fifty families who had suffered similar losses. This contrasted with a records request to the UK Office of National Statistics, which showed only twenty-one out of tens of thousands of suicide files in England and Wales mentioned the terms "gamble" or "gambling" between 2001 and 2016.

In 2018, the Ritchies founded Gambling with Lives, a charity to build gambling-related suicide awareness and fight for policy changes in the United Kingdom. It wants "all gambling-related suicides to be reported, investigated and recorded" by coroners. It also offers support services for those who have lost loved ones to gambling-related suicides. The Ritchies' work has brought these deaths to the forefront of UK gambling debates, influencing policy as the government made updates to its 2005 Gambling Act to reflect modern realities like online gambling.

Leading medical journal *The Lancet Public Health* has lauded the group for highlighting "the widespread and devastating impact of gambling-related suicides, and the lack of effective responses from government, regulators, and industry." Among the reforms the government has enacted in response to the advocacy of Gambling with Lives are operator prompts to set financial deposit limits, maximum online stake limits (£5 per spin for gamblers twenty-five and older and £2 per spin for those eighteen to twenty-four) and a statutory levy on operators licensed by the United Kingdom. They must pay 1.1 percent of the gross gambling yield to fund gambling prevention, research, and treatment initiatives. From 2000 to

2012, Ontario collected a 2 percent levy from most slot machines in the province to put toward similar aims, but only Alberta's new iGaming industry collects such a levy today, valued at 1 percent of gross gambling revenues.

Most notably, Gambling with Lives has made headway with the coronial system in the United Kingdom. Since 2022, with representation from the law firm Leigh Day, it has helped families navigate the coronial inquest process. Six suicide deaths have since had gambling recorded as a contributing factor. Unlike normal death investigations, inquests involve fact-finding beyond the normal scope, calling evidence and witnesses and determining, as Dr. Bowes would put it, "the great why" in order to recommend how to prevent other similar suicides. (At least four have taken place in Australia since 2010 as well.)

Reports are released to "interested persons," people, government departments, and other organizations who can act to prevent further such deaths. In the case of Luke Ashton, a forty-year-old father from Leicester, one of the world's largest betting companies, Betfair, was deemed an "interested person," reportedly for the first time. This resulted in Betfair making several policy updates, including monthly deposit limits for all customers returning from self-exclusion periods and a £10 stake limit for online slot games. The coroner listed "gambling disorder" as a secondary cause of Luke's 2021 death—reportedly a UK first—and different from how it is typically recorded, which is as a risk factor, at best.

The upcoming eleventh update for the International Classification of Diseases—the codes used worldwide to indicate medical diagnoses and causes of death—might further open discussion. It assigns codes to gambling disorder for the first time. In theory, this allows it to be included on death certificates in a consistent manner. The Canadian Institute for Health Information, which works with StatsCan on ICD-11 adoption in Canada, says assessment is underway on implementing the updates, but a date is unknown. As coding rules are decided by provinces and territories, there is no guarantee that codes for gambling disorder will be used consistently or at all by Canadian coroners and medical examiners. If they did follow the new code rules, it could help further simplify the tracking of gambling as a suicide risk factor and make the application more consistent.

Based on an evidence review, Public Health England now has a formal, if broad, estimate of gambling-related suicides in the country. It estimates between 117 and 496 gambling-related suicides occur annually in England, or between 2.35 and 9.98 percent of suicides. Of all data provided to me by provinces, only five instances from 2000 to 2023 fell in this range. PHAC says it "does not estimate how many suicide deaths per year are attributable to any single risk factor," and provincial and territorial public health agencies don't keep estimates of the prevalence of gambling-related suicides, either.

* * *

It's no wonder stories of gambling harms, including suicides, abound in Australia. It has some of the world's highest per-capita gambling rates. Despite having only 1 percent of the world's population, Australia is reported to have 20 percent of the world's VLTs (known Down Under as "pokies"). With about $25 billion (AUD) wagered annually, Aussies gamble about double what Canadians do in legal markets. A recent paper by Australian researchers surveyed gamblers and reported they found gambling to be an important part of the country's culture.

"This exaggerated perception of engagement in gambling is a concern as research from other areas of public health, such as tobacco and alcohol, shows that people are more likely to engage in the consumption of harmful products when they perceive that this is a normal, socially accepted and culturally endorsed activity," write the researchers in the *Australian and New Zealand Journal of Public Health.*

On the first day he opened his account with the bookmaker CrownBet, Christopher, a middle-aged, newly divorced man, deposited nearly $207,000 AUD. Within five weeks he gambled away $355,014.49 AUD. Despite his massive losses, and only $0.79 AUD remaining in his bank account, the company didn't contact him.

Christopher (a pseudonym) spoke with a *Sydney Morning Herald* journalist and with Financial Counselling Australia, a nonprofit organization aimed at reducing financial hardship, to share his gambling experiences. He hoped doing so could improve policy outcomes. A few months after speaking with FCA, Christopher died by suicide. In the weeks following his death, his family learned he had lost more than $500,000 gambling. According to a report from the nonprofit, "Christopher's death wasn't captured in the coronial gambling reporting process."

His death prompted a policy roundtable with representatives from thirty organizations, the likes of which have never been seen in Canada. It included coroners' courts from two Australian states, representation from the prime minister's cabinet, major banks, mental health professionals, and even a gambling firm. They discussed next steps to reducing deaths like Christopher's.

The top recommendation in *Gambling and Suicide Prevention—A Roadmap for Change* was identifying and recording gambling-related suicides by "consciously [looking] for problematic gambling as a contributing factor," as opposed to the passive methods used by most coroners and medical examiners (including Canada's) of recording the information only if it came up. The roundtable suggested the data needs to be captured nationally and included publicly in suicide datasets, and that the federal government should establish a national gambling-related suicide prevention plan. To date none of this has happened.

Recently, FCA has started lobbying for data vaults in the Australian gambling industry. The vaults are safe servers where regulators can access the information of bettors, which may use reference numbers to retain anonymity. Regulators can use this data in several ways critical to their missions, including to monitor self-exclusion, identify harmful play patterns, or deposits which may put customers at risk, or those that represent potential money-laundering. It would also be possible for governments to review the records of people who have died by suicide to scan for problematic gambling habits. At least fifteen countries have data vaults, including Denmark, France, and Spain. Private companies have no choice but to participate in the data vault scheme, as jurisdictions make it a condition of gambling licence agreements.

Discussion of data vaults hasn't reached Canada yet, although Ontario is provided certain anonymized data by iGaming partners. This is yet another example of how far behind Canada is in securing the sort of gambling data that can help prevent addictions and, in turn, gambling-related suicides.

* * *

When looking for solutions to the human costs of gambling, the perfect is the enemy of the good. There's been enough pushback on gambling-related suicides—that they can't be tracked, for example, or quibbling over whether they're worth recording—that we've missed out on the incremental progress that could otherwise have helped people.

Coroner and medical examiner offices, the people with the closest access to the information, have been reluctant to lead reforms. Manitoba's chief medical examiner Dr. John Younes says the province is open to changing how it tracks suicide data if there are new national best practices or standards to follow. Put another way, his office isn't going to make changes unless someone tells him to or everyone else decides to. If every coroner or medical examiner office takes the same tack, reform will come at a snail's pace.

One tool at the disposal of Canadian coroner and medical examiner offices is the inquest. Most have authority to perform them. They are frequently held over several days, and sometimes known by other terms such as fatality inquiries. Dr. Matthew Bowes, chief medical examiner of Nova Scotia, notes that his office can only *recommend* inquiries, which are resource-intensive and rare—only four have taken place since 2000. For deaths in hospitals, prisons, or workplaces, inquests are typically mandatory. But most coroners and medical examiners can order inquests if they believe public interest exists—if the way someone died can affect a swath of the population. Inquests include making recommendations to provincial governments, which must be acknowledged, responded to, and used to revisit policies.

In 2010, Ontario's coroner office completed an inquest into the suicide of eighteen-year-old Sara Carlin to review the circumstances of her death, and, more broadly, links between antidepressant use and teenage suicides. With 6 percent of Canadians using prescription antidepressants—a figure similar to the rate of adults who are at risk for or have gambling problems, according to CCHS data and expert estimates of gambling-related suicide prevalence—it suggests there are similar public interest arguments to be made. But no Canadian gambling-related suicide has resulted in an inquest.

Dr. Bowes thinks death review committees are a better fit than inquests for understanding gambling-related suicides. Nova Scotia launched such committees in 2023, chaired by Bowes and made up of subject matter experts and community members, to analyze particular types of deaths—like those of children or incidents related to domestic violence. Committees have power to obtain the deceased's health records and produce public annual reports with their findings. "More importantly, they're given a specific mandate to explore the causative factors and to make recommendations to prevent those kinds of deaths in the future," Bowes says.

In September 2025, the first annual report of Nova Scotia's Child Death Review Committee was released, which reviewed deaths of youth under age twenty-five in the province between 2009 and 2023. Among the 911 deaths, contributing factors and trends were identified "including sudden infant death syndrome, suicide, and motor vehicle crashes." One recommendation was "enhancing collaboration on suicide and homicide prevention among high-risk groups." Though all provinces currently have at least one death review committee, none presently focuses on gambling-related suicides.

In New Brunswick, the 2024 pilot of a suicide fatality review committee coincided with the development of a new Coroners Office form to capture information from death investigations. "The new form requires the capture of information related to potential gambling issues, and this will allow the committee to better assess the impact of gambling addictions as a suicide factor," says David Kelly, a New Brunswick Department of Health communications officer. Coroner Services quietly implemented the new protocol in January 2024 and by December of that year had already captured one gambling-related suicide using the new system. Prior to that, it had recorded one such death since 2017.

In mid-November 2025, about a year after my first investigations into gambling-related suicides were published, Newfoundland and Labrador's Office of the Chief Medical Examiner began collecting data on gambling as a risk factor for suicide. The office says "[t]here is also on-going retrospective data collection for all suicides for the period of November 15, 2024-November 15, 2025." A freedom of information request shows that 'history of gambling' is part of a stressors checklist.

Angela Rintoul, principal research fellow of gambling and suicide at the University of Melbourne, says an imperfect system is better than none. "You've got to start somewhere," she says, as long as inefficiencies are identified and best practices evolve and improve.

The definition of "gambling-related" is key to understanding the process, says Rintoul. In Canada, suicides that coroners or medical examiners associate with gambling as a risk factor generally fall into two categories: gambling is mentioned in a suicide note or directly in interviews with those close to the deceased. Unlike alcohol or drugs, which coroner or medical examiners can test for post-mortem, gambling is invisible. "There's no biomarker," Rintoul says. "Before you get to the coroner's office, you also want to be tracking a whole lot of other indicators in society."

This includes recording diagnoses of gambling disorder in medical files, as well as how many people call helplines in suicidal distress because of gambling, or make emergency room visits or ambulance calls for gambling-related suicide attempts. All these data points can help inform suicide prevention rather than "postvention" efforts.

There are more general changes that governments could implement to keep Canadian gamblers safer. For instance, passing legislation, such as the proposed Bill S-211, which will regulate sports betting advertising at the federal level. Canada could also follow Australia's lead in not letting people bet online using credit cards. And there could be limits set on betting levels—no sound reason exists for a government to allow players the option of betting $10,000 on a single spin of an online machine. In the past, part of the trepidation around reforming product design has been revenue concerns. For instance, when Nova Scotia lost $47.5 million in VLT revenues after introducing technology that let gamblers track their play, the government pulled the plug.

* * *

We are at a crossroads. No rational person looks at the state of gambling in Canada and thinks only about whether profits will be affected by changes. The issue must be viewed holistically. Some Canadians will see any clawback or restriction of the industry as a form of nanny state, but gambling reforms are not designed to coddle adults, keeping them from spending their money as they want to. It is less paternalism than prudence. Keeping gambling in check keeps people healthy and financially sound, and reduces the spinoff damage to their partners, kids, and other loved ones, as well as their workplaces and communities.

As lotteries spread in the 1980s, there was evidence some people became heavy, compulsive players. Economists suggested the games were an informal tax on low-income players, who bought more tickets but also spent greater portions of their earnings relative to others. "A $10 outlay on lottery tickets is 5 percent of a busboy's $200 weekly income, but only 1 percent of a mid-level executive's $1,000," observed one reporter in 1989. The tickets began to resemble a regressive tax, where rates are flat but the spend takes a bigger portion of a lower earner's income. University of Alberta economics professor John Livernois estimated lottery revenues were collected twice as regressively as average retail sales taxes, but his assertion didn't create significant outrage.

Today, there is still evidence that certain populations are affected differently by gambling. While more Canadians in the highest-income households gamble than in the lowest (71.5 percent versus 53.8 percent), only 1.1 percent of these wealthier Canadians faced moderate-to-severe risk of gambling problems. Yet 2.7 percent of the least affluent households faced a problem. Worse still, the lower-income households spend a larger share of their discretionary income. The barrage of widespread gambling options makes life more miserable for some segments of the population who are already marginalized. This includes, according to StatCan, non-white and Indigenous people, the LGBTQ community, even people with "fair or poor" self-perceptions of mental health as opposed to "good, very good or excellent."

This is a critical time to pause and reconsider whether we're comfortable with the gambling industry and its ways. It appears that lawmakers and citizens alike didn't realize how intrusive gambling would become with the latest wave of sports and digital options. The ads and billboards littering cities and the internet, the sports fans bombarded with promotions when they try to unwind and watch their favourite team, the betting odds discussed in the news as casually as the weather, the gambling-like prediction markets that are starting to creep in to life outside sports, enabling people to wager on all sorts of real-world events, from stock trends to war outcomes. It feels like having someone in your ear, pressuring you to join in.

This can't be disconnected from the broader economic environment of stagnant incomes and limited opportunities. People who feel their chances for an economically secure life are waning are more vulnerable laying down bets, even if they know the house always wins. It's the same mentality that keeps people buying the latest crypto "shitcoin" or meme stock. Making a dozen sports bets on a single game just in case one or two hit, putting it all on red or black in the online casino—it might pay off huge in an instant. When your dreams have been priced out of reach, what's one more loss? It's understandable that regular people may not feel they have the power to make the changes required to live economically rewarding lives, but should governments be actively promoting behaviours that make those lives even harder?

We need not rid ourselves of the gambling industry wholesale to live in a world where addictions can be minimized, gambling-related suicides can be prevented, and lives saved. It is possible for Canada to allow legal gambling and still steer people away from the worst consequences of over-indulgence. The time has arrived to try.

The first step is to accept that an inevitable consequence of a massive gambling industry is that some people will get in over their heads and deaths will happen. We can't be certain of how many, given the challenges in accurately counting suicides. But we can be certain that the link between gambling and suicides is real. In the eyes of those most severely afflicted—including compulsive gamblers who have considered suicide, bereaved families and the deceased who leave suicide letters—the connection is real. That's what matters most. If the industry continues expanding and addiction rates continue rising, new groups of Canadians—some of whom may never consider taking their lives until they become addicted to gambling—may attempt or die by suicide. We need resources in place to help before this happens.

The most dire consequences of gambling addiction can be prevented and we have the infrastructure in Canada to do so. But right now, the priority of our provincial governments is cashing in on the gambling boom. They need to make room for other priorities. If governments lead the way with money and action, others will follow. There is already energy and resources put toward identifying who is at risk for suicide and showing them another way forward. What's missing is the acknowledgement that some of these people are addicted to gambling and that governments are abetting destructive behaviour. We need suicide prevention methods targeted directly at gamblers.

Our provinces need to direct coroners and medical examiners to pay particular attention to gambling as a factor in suicides, track the information as diligently as they can, and share relevant information with stakeholders in the fight to save lives. I know firsthand from reading Quebec's suicide investigation files that when enough information is put in a report and available to those who can use it, there are enough commonalities to identify who may be at risk. It's possible to view these people as an identifiable group and develop strategies to help them.

If harm reduction requires gambling corporations to proactively enforce play limits, lower maximum bets for online casinos, add friction to seamless onboarding processes, and intervene with players who lose large amounts of money quickly, we'll all be better off. The companies want to be in the market at any cost, and they will make sacrifices to do it, but they won't do so on their own. "Nobody's going to want to unilaterally disarm in the competition for more customers," a sports book manager with Hard Rock Digital told a 2026 panel audience. Lawmakers and regulators will have to push these companies to, and in the case of provincially owned gambling products, themselves. The purpose of having governments regulate gambling is to *regulate* it, not squeeze every last dollar out of citizens.

Canada's journey from a modest gambling industry to one with nearly inescapable reach has been dotted with missed opportunities to stop harms. Canadians across generations have lost their money, their homes, their families, their jobs, and their self-worth. Some unknown number have lost their lives. Their stories have always been written in invisible ink on the annual reports which boast about climbing gambling revenues.

Canada can take a leadership role now, setting an example for other nations. Provincial and national stakeholders can create solutions to limit the human costs of gambling.

We have failed these people in the past, but it doesn't have to be our future. The best we can do for them is to ensure their suffering didn't go unnoticed. That their warnings are listened to now, even if we should have listened to them sooner.

ABOUT THE AUTHOR

Rob Csernyik is Canada's most distinguished journalist on the gambling beat. His reporting on the economic and social consequences of gambling has won prizes from the Atlantic Journalism Awards, Digital Publishing Awards, and RTDNA Canada. In 2022 he was awarded a Michener-Deacon Fellowship for Investigative Reporting to research gambling-related suicides.